Mindful
of the Body

A STUDY GUIDE

prepared by

Thanissaro Bhikkhu

for free distribution

Contents

Introduction

ALTHOUGH EARLY BUDDHISM is widely believed to take a negative attitude toward the body, the texts of the Pali Canon do not support this belief. They approach the body both in its positive role, as an object of meditation to develop mindfulness, concentration, and the mental powers based on concentration; and in its negative role as an object for unskillful states of mind. Even in its negative role, the body is not the culprit: the problem is the mind's attachment to the body. Once the body can be used in its positive role to develop mindfulness and concentration, those mental qualities can be used to free the mind of its attachments to the body. Then, as many a modern meditation master has noted, the mind and body can live in peace.

This study guide focuses on the primary sutta in the Pali Canon dealing with the contemplation of the body: The Discourse on Mindfulness Immersed in the Body (MN 119). The first section, The Context, establishes the general principles underlying the practice of mindfulness immersed in the body, showing why attachment to the body is considered problematic in the first place. The second section presents the sutta itself. The remaining sections expand on points raised in the sutta: Section Three dealing with the advantages of practicing mindfulness immersed in the body, and Section Four expanding on the drawbacks of attachment to the body.

Because the sutta treats the body both as an object of mindfulness and as an object of *jhana*, or mental absorption, it raises questions concerning the relationship between these two mental qualities in the practice of meditation.

There is a widespread belief that they represent two sides of a great divide in Buddhist meditation practice, with mindfulness on one side, joined with *vipassana* (insight) and discernment; and jhana on the other side joined with *samatha* (tranquility). The Pali Canon, however, presents a much more complex picture of the interrelated roles these mental qualities in the pursuit of Awakening. And in fact, the "Great Divide" picture of Buddhist meditation practice conflates what the Pali Canon treats as three separate, albeit related issues: the relationship between samatha and vipassana, the relationship between mindfulness and jhana, and the relationship between jhana and discernment.

To convey the original parameters of these issues, this study guide ends with three sections focused separately on these relationships. The first, Samatha/Vipassana, shows how these terms refer not to separate classes of meditative exercises but to qualities of mind that ideally are developed in tandem as a necessary part of jhana practice—both prior to and building on the attainment of jhana. The next section, Mindfulness/Jhana, similarly shows how the practice of jhana and the practice of the four establishings of mindfulness—also called the four frames of reference—are not radically separate. Instead, mindfulness practice is used specifically to develop jhana, whereas jhana practice—on the attainment of the fourth jhana—brings mindfulness to a state of purity. The final section, Jhana/Discernment—shows how the attainment of jhana is used as a necessary basis for the development of liberating insight. This section concludes with a passage from MN 121 that ties all these themes together, showing how tranquility and insight mindfully act in tandem (see AN IV.94) to develop and purify jhana states in such a way as to foster the discernment that issues in release.

I. The Context

"Monks, I lived in refinement, utmost refinement, total refinement. My father even had lotus ponds made in our palace: one where red-lotuses bloomed, one where white lotuses bloomed, one where blue lotuses bloomed, all for my sake. I used no sandalwood that was not from Varanasi. My turban was from Varanasi, as were my tunic, my lower garments, & my outer cloak. A white sunshade was held over me day & night to protect me from cold, heat, dust, dirt, & dew.

"I had three palaces: one for the cold season, one for the hot season, one for the rainy season. During the four months of the rainy season I was entertained in the rainy-season palace by minstrels without a single man among them, and I did not once come down from the palace. Whereas the servants, workers, & retainers in other people's homes are fed meals of lentil soup & broken rice, in my father's home the servants, workers, & retainers were fed wheat, rice, and meat.

"Even though I was endowed with such fortune, such total refinement, the thought occurred to me: 'When an untaught, run-of-the-mill person, himself subject to aging, not beyond aging, sees another who is aged, he is horrified, humiliated, & disgusted, oblivious to himself that he too is subject to aging, not beyond aging. If I—who am subject to aging, not beyond aging—were to be horrified, humiliated, & disgusted on seeing another person who is aged, that would not be fitting for me.' As I noticed this, the [typical] young person's intoxication with youth entirely dropped away.

"Even though I was endowed with such fortune, such total refinement, the thought occurred to me: 'When an untaught, run-of-the-mill person, himself subject to illness, not beyond illness, sees another who is ill, he is horrified, humiliated, & disgusted, oblivious to himself that he too is subject to illness, not beyond illness. And if I—who am subject to illness, not beyond illness—were to be horrified, humiliated, & disgusted on seeing another person who is ill, that would not be fitting for me.' As I noticed this, the healthy person's intoxication with health entirely dropped away.

"Even though I was endowed with such fortune, such total refinement, the thought occurred to me: 'When an untaught, run-of-the-mill person, himself subject to death, not beyond death, sees another who is dead, he is horrified, humiliated, & disgusted, oblivious to himself that he too is subject to death, not beyond death. And if I—who am subject to death, not beyond death—were to be horrified, humiliated, & disgusted on seeing another person who is dead, that would not be fitting for me.' As I noticed this, the living person's intoxication with life entirely dropped away.

"Monks, there are these three forms of intoxication. Which three? Intoxication with youth, intoxication with health, intoxication with life.

"Drunk with the intoxication of youth, an uninstructed, run-of-the-mill person engages in bodily misconduct, verbal misconduct, & mental misconduct. Having engaged in bodily misconduct, verbal misconduct, & mental misconduct, he—on the break-up of the body, after death—reappears in the plane of deprivation, the bad destination, the lower realms, in hell.

"Drunk with the intoxication of health, an uninstructed, run-of-the-mill person engages in bodily misconduct, verbal misconduct, & mental misconduct. Having engaged in bodily misconduct, verbal misconduct, & mental misconduct, he—on the break-up of the body, after death—reappears in the plane of deprivation, the bad destination, the lower realms, in hell.

"Drunk with the intoxication of life, an uninstructed, run-of-the-mill person engages in bodily misconduct, verbal misconduct, & mental misconduct. Having engaged in bodily misconduct, verbal misconduct, & mental misconduct, he—on the break-up of the body, after death—reappears in the plane of deprivation, the bad destination, the lower realms, in hell...."

—AN III.39

"Before my Awakening, when I was still an unawakened Bodhisatta, being subject myself to birth, aging, illness, death, sorrow, and defilement, I sought [happiness in] what was subject to birth, aging, illness, death, sorrow, and defilement. The thought occurred to me: 'Why am I, being subject myself to birth...defilement, seeking what is subject to birth...defilement? What if I...were to seek the unborn, unaging, unailing, undying, sorrowless, undefiled, unsurpassed security from bondage: Unbinding.'"

—MN 26

"I tell you, friend, that it isn't possible by traveling to know or see or reach a far end of the cosmos where one doesn't take birth, age, die, pass away, or reappear. But at the same time, I tell you that there is no making an end of suffering & stress without reaching the end of the cosmos. Yet it is just within this fathom-long body, with its perception & intellect, that I declare that there is the cosmos, the origination of the cosmos, the cessation of the cosmos, and the path of practice leading to the cessation of the cosmos."

—AN IV.45

"Now this is the noble truth of stress: Birth is stressful, aging is stressful, death is stressful; sorrow, lamentation, pain, distress, & despair are stressful; association with the unbeloved is stressful, separation from the loved is stressful, not getting what is wanted is stressful. In short, the five clinging-aggregates are stressful.

"And this is the noble truth of the origination of stress: the craving that makes for further becoming—accompanied by passion & delight, relishing now here & now there—i.e., craving for sensuality, craving for becoming, craving for non-becoming.

"And this is the noble truth of the cessation of stress: the remainderless fading & cessation, renunciation, relinquishment, release, & letting go of that very craving.

"And this is the noble truth of the way of practice leading to the cessation of stress: precisely this Noble Eightfold Path—right view, right resolve, right speech, right action, right livelihood, right effort, right mindfulness, right concentration.

"'This noble truth of stress is to be comprehended' ... 'This noble truth of the origination of stress is to be abandoned' ... 'This noble truth of the cessation of stress is to be directly experienced' ... 'This noble truth of the way of practice leading to the cessation of stress is to be developed' ...."

—SN LVI.11

"And what, monks, is right view? Knowledge with regard to stress, knowledge with regard to the origination of stress, knowledge with regard to the stopping of stress, knowledge with regard to the way of practice leading to the stopping of stress: This, monks, is called right view.

"And what, monks, is right resolve? Being resolved on renunciation, on freedom from ill will, on harmlessness: This, monks, is called right resolve.

"And what, monks, is right speech? Abstaining from lying, abstaining from divisive speech, abstaining from abusive speech, abstaining from idle chatter: This, monks, is called right speech.

"And what, monks, is right action? Abstaining from taking life, abstaining from stealing, abstaining from sexual intercourse: This, monks, is called right action.

"And what, monks, is right livelihood? There is the case where a disciple of the noble ones, having abandoned dishonest livelihood, keeps his life going with right livelihood: This, monks, is called right livelihood.

"And what, monks, is right effort? (i) There is the case where a monk generates desire, endeavors, activates persistence, upholds & exerts his intent for the sake of the non-arising of evil, unskillful qualities that have not yet arisen. (ii) He generates desire, endeavors, activates persistence, upholds & exerts his intent for the sake of the abandonment of evil, unskillful qualities that have arisen. (iii) He generates desire, endeavors, activates persistence, upholds & exerts his intent for the sake of the arising of skillful qualities that have not yet arisen. (iv) He generates desire, endeavors, activates persistence, upholds & exerts his intent for the maintenance, non-confusion, increase, plenitude, development, & culmination of skillful qualities that have arisen: This, monks, is called right effort.

"And what, monks, is right mindfulness? (i) There is the case where a monk remains focused on the body in & of itself—ardent, aware, & mindful—putting away greed & distress with reference to the world. (ii) He remains focused on feelings in & of themselves—ardent, aware, & mindful—putting away greed & distress with reference to the world. (iii) He remains focused on the mind in & of itself—ardent, aware, & mindful—putting away greed & distress with reference to the world. (iv) He remains focused on mental qualities in & of themselves—ardent, aware, & mindful—

putting away greed & distress with reference to the world. This, monks, is called right mindfulness.

"And what, monks, is right concentration? (i) There is the case where a monk—quite withdrawn from sensuality, withdrawn from unskillful (mental) qualities—enters & remains in the first jhana: rapture & pleasure born from withdrawal, accompanied by directed thought & evaluation. (ii) With the stilling of directed thought & evaluation, he enters & remains in the second jhana: rapture & pleasure born of concentration, unification of awareness free from directed thought & evaluation—internal assurance. (iii) With the fading of rapture, he remains in equanimity, mindful & fully aware, and physically sensitive of pleasure. He enters & remains in the third jhana, of which the Noble Ones declare, 'Equanimous & mindful, he has a pleasurable abiding.' (iv) With the abandoning of pleasure & pain—as with the earlier disappearance of elation & distress—he enters & remains in the fourth jhana: purity of equanimity & mindfulness, neither pleasure nor pain. This, monks, is called right concentration."

—*SN XLV.8*

II. Mindfulness Immersed in the Body

Kāyagatā-sati Sutta (Majjhima Nikāya 119)

I have heard that on one occasion the Blessed One was staying in Savatthi at Jeta's Grove, Anathapindika's monastery. Now at that time a large number of monks, after the meal, on returning from their alms round, had gathered at the meeting hall when this discussion arose: "Isn't it amazing, friends! Isn't it astounding!—the extent to which mindfulness immersed in the body, when developed & pursued, is said by the Blessed One who knows, who sees—the worthy one, rightly self-awakened—to be of great fruit & great benefit." And this discussion came to no conclusion.

Then the Blessed One, emerging from his seclusion in the late afternoon, went to the meeting hall and, on arrival, sat down on a seat made ready. As he was sitting there, he addressed the monks: "For what topic are you gathered together here? And what was the discussion that came to no conclusion?"

"Just now, lord, after the meal, on returning from our alms round, we gathered at the meeting hall when this discussion arose: 'Isn't it amazing, friends! Isn't it astounding!—the extent to which mindfulness immersed in the body, when developed & pursued, is said by the Blessed One who knows, who sees—the worthy one, rightly self-awakened—to be of great fruit & great benefit.' This was the discussion that had come to no conclusion when the Blessed One arrived."

[The Blessed One said:] "And how is mindfulness immersed in the body developed, how is it pursued, so as to be of great fruit & great benefit?

"There is the case where a monk—having gone to the wilderness, to the shade of a tree, or to an empty building— sits down folding his legs crosswise, holding his body erect and setting mindfulness to the fore. Always mindful, he breathes in; mindful he breathes out.

"Breathing in long, he discerns that he is breathing in long; or breathing out long, he discerns that he is breathing out long. Or breathing in short, he discerns that he is breathing in short; or breathing out short, he discerns that he is breathing out short. He trains himself to breathe in sensitive to the entire body and to breathe out sensitive to the entire body. He trains himself to breathe in calming bodily fabrication (the breath) and to breathe out calming bodily fabrication. And as he remains thus heedful, ardent, & resolute, any memories & resolves related to the household life are abandoned, and with their abandoning his mind gathers & settles inwardly, grows unified & centered. This is how a monk develops mindfulness immersed in the body.

"Furthermore, when walking, the monk discerns that he is walking. When standing, he discerns that he is standing. When sitting, he discerns that he is sitting. When lying down, he discerns that he is lying down. Or however his body is disposed, that is how he discerns it. And as he remains thus heedful, ardent, & resolute, any memories & resolves related to the household life are abandoned, and with their abandoning his mind gathers & settles inwardly, grows unified & centered. This is how a monk develops mindfulness immersed in the body.

"Furthermore, when going forward & returning, he makes himself fully alert; when looking toward & looking away...when bending & extending his limbs...when carrying his outer cloak, his upper robe & his bowl...when eating, drinking, chewing, & savoring...when urinating & defecating...when walking, standing, sitting, falling asleep, waking up, talking, & remaining silent, he makes himself fully alert. And as he remains thus heedful, ardent, & resolute, any memories & resolves related to the household life are abandoned, and with their abandoning his mind gathers & settles inwardly, grows unified & centered. This is how a monk develops mindfulness immersed in the body.

"Furthermore, the monk reflects on this very body from the soles of the feet on up, from the crown of the head on down, surrounded by skin and full of various kinds of unclean things: 'In this body there are head hairs, body hairs, nails, teeth, skin, flesh, tendons, bones, bone marrow, kidneys, heart, liver, pleura, spleen, lungs, large intestines, small intestines, gorge, feces, bile, phlegm, pus, blood, sweat, fat, tears, skin-oil, saliva, mucus, fluid in the joints, urine.' Just as if a sack with openings at both ends were full of various kinds of grain—wheat, rice, mung beans, kidney beans, sesame seeds, husked rice—and a man with good eyesight, pouring it out, were to reflect, 'This is wheat. This is rice. These are mung beans. These are kidney beans. These are sesame seeds. This is husked rice'; in the same way, the monk reflects on this very body from the soles of the feet on up, from the crown of the head on down, surrounded by skin and full of various kinds of unclean things: 'In this body there are head hairs, body hairs, nails, teeth, skin, flesh, tendons, bones, bone marrow, kidneys, heart, liver, pleura, spleen, lungs, large intestines, small intestines, gorge, feces, bile, phlegm, pus, blood, sweat, fat, tears, skin-oil, saliva, mucus, fluid in the joints, urine.' And as he remains thus heedful, ardent, & resolute, any memories & resolves related to the household life are abandoned, and with their abandoning his mind gathers & settles inwardly, grows unified & centered. This is how a monk develops mindfulness immersed in the body.

"Furthermore, the monk contemplates this very body—however it stands, however it is disposed—in terms of properties: 'In this body there is the earth property, the liquid property, the fire property, & the wind property.' Just as a skilled butcher or his apprentice, having killed a cow, would sit at a crossroads cutting it up into pieces, the monk contemplates this very body—however it stands, however it is disposed—in terms of properties: 'In this body there is the earth property, the liquid property, the fire property, & the wind property.' And as he remains thus heedful, ardent, & resolute, any memories & resolves related to the household life are abandoned, and with their abandoning his mind gathers & settles inwardly, grows unified & centered. This is how a monk develops mindfulness immersed in the body.

"Furthermore, as if he were to see a corpse cast away in a charnel ground—one day, two days, three days dead—bloated, livid, & festering, he applies it to this very body, 'This body, too: Such is its nature, such is its future, such its unavoidable fate'...

"Or again, as if he were to see a corpse cast away in a charnel ground, picked at by crows, vultures, & hawks, by dogs, hyenas, & various other creatures...a skeleton smeared with flesh & blood, connected with tendons...a fleshless skeleton smeared with blood, connected with tendons...a skeleton without flesh or blood, connected with tendons...bones detached from their tendons, scattered in all directions—here a hand bone, there a foot bone, here a shin bone, there a thigh bone, here a hip bone, there a back bone, here a rib, there a chest bone, here a shoulder bone, there a neck bone, here a jaw bone, there a tooth, here a skull...the bones whitened, somewhat like the color of shells...piled up, more than a year old...decomposed into a powder: He applies it to this very body, 'This body, too: Such is its nature, such is its future, such its unavoidable fate.'

"And as he remains thus heedful, ardent, & resolute, any memories & resolves related to the household life are abandoned, and with their abandoning his mind gathers & settles inwardly, grows unified & centered. This is how a monk develops mindfulness immersed in the body.

THE FOUR JHANAS

"Furthermore, quite withdrawn from sensual pleasures, withdrawn from unskillful mental qualities, he enters & remains in the first jhana: rapture & pleasure born from withdrawal, accompanied by directed thought & evaluation. He permeates & pervades, suffuses & fills this very body with the rapture & pleasure born from withdrawal. Just as if a skilled bathman or bathman's apprentice would pour bath powder into a brass basin and knead it together, sprinkling it again & again with water, so that his ball of bath powder—saturated, moisture-laden, permeated within & without—would nevertheless not drip; even so, the monk permeates ... this very body with the rapture & pleasure born of withdrawal. There is nothing of his entire body unpervaded by rapture & pleasure born from withdrawal. And as he remains thus heedful, ardent, & resolute, any memories & resolves related to the household life are abandoned, and with their abandoning his mind gathers & settles inwardly, grows unified & centered. This is how a monk develops mindfulness immersed in the body.

"Then, with the stilling of directed thought & evaluation, he enters & remains in the second jhana: rapture & pleasure born of composure, unification of awareness free from directed thought & evaluation—internal assurance. He permeates & pervades, suffuses & fills this very body with the rapture & pleasure born of composure. Just like a lake with spring-water welling up from within, having no inflow from the east, west, north, or south, and with the skies supplying abundant showers time & again, so that

the cool fount of water welling up from within the lake
would permeate & pervade, suffuse & fill it with cool
waters, there being no part of the lake unpervaded by the
cool waters; even so, the monk permeates ... this very body
with the rapture & pleasure born of composure. There is
nothing of his entire body unpervaded by rapture & pleasure born of composure. And as he remains thus heedful,
ardent, & resolute, any memories & resolves related to the
household life are abandoned, and with their abandoning
his mind gathers & settles inwardly, grows unified &
centered. This is how a monk develops mindfulness
immersed in the body.

"Then, with the fading of rapture, he remains in equanimity, mindful & alert, and physically sensitive of
pleasure. He enters & remains in the third jhana, of which
the noble ones declare, 'Equanimous & mindful, he has a
pleasurable abiding.' He permeates & pervades, suffuses &
fills this very body with the pleasure divested of rapture.
Just as in a lotus pond, some of the lotuses, born & growing
in the water, stay immersed in the water and flourish without standing up out of the water, so that they are permeated
& pervaded, suffused & filled with cool water from their
roots to their tips, and nothing of those lotuses would be
unpervaded with cool water; even so, the monk permeates
... this very body with the pleasure divested of rapture.
There is nothing of his entire body unpervaded with pleasure divested of rapture. And as he remains thus heedful,
ardent, & resolute, any memories & resolves related to the
household life are abandoned, and with their abandoning
his mind gathers & settles inwardly, grows unified &
centered. This is how a monk develops mindfulness
immersed in the body.

"Then, with the abandoning of pleasure & pain—as
with the earlier disappearance of elation & distress—he
enters & remains in the fourth jhana: purity of equanimity &

mindfulness, neither-pleasure-nor-pain. He sits, permeating the body with a pure, bright awareness. Just as if a man were sitting covered from head to foot with a white cloth so that there would be no part of his body to which the white cloth did not extend; even so, the monk sits, permeating the body with a pure, bright awareness. There is nothing of his entire body unpervaded by pure, bright awareness. And as he remains thus heedful, ardent, & resolute, any memories & resolves related to the household life are abandoned, and with their abandoning his mind gathers & settles inwardly, grows unified & centered. This is how a monk develops mindfulness immersed in the body.

FULLNESS OF MIND

"Monks, whoever develops & pursues mindfulness immersed in the body encompasses whatever skillful qualities are on the side of clear knowing. Just as whoever pervades the great ocean with his awareness encompasses whatever rivulets flow down into the ocean, in the same way, whoever develops & pursues mindfulness immersed in the body encompasses whatever skillful qualities are on the side of clear knowing.

"In whomever mindfulness immersed in the body is not developed, not pursued, Mara gains entry, Mara gains a foothold.

"Suppose that a man were to throw a heavy stone ball into a pile of wet clay. What do you think, monks—would the heavy stone ball gain entry into the pile of wet clay?"

"Yes, venerable sir."

"In the same way, in whomever mindfulness immersed in the body is not developed, not pursued, Mara gains entry, Mara gains a foothold.

"Now, suppose that there were a dry, sapless piece of timber, and a man were to come along with an upper fire-stick, thinking, 'I'll light a fire. I'll produce heat.' What do you think—would he be able to light a fire and produce heat by rubbing the upper fire-stick in the dry, sapless piece of timber?"

"Yes, venerable sir."

"In the same way, in whomever mindfulness immersed in the body is not developed, not pursued, Mara gains entry, Mara gains a foothold.

"Now, suppose that there were an empty, hollow water-pot set on a stand, and a man were to come along carrying a load of water. What do you think—would he get a place to put his water?"

"Yes, venerable sir."

"In the same way, in whomever mindfulness immersed in the body is not developed, not pursued, Mara gains entry, Mara gains a foothold.

"Now, in whomever mindfulness immersed in the body is developed, is pursued, Mara gains no entry, Mara gains no foothold. Suppose that a man were to throw a ball of string against a door panel made entirely of heartwood. What do you think—would that light ball of string gain entry into that door panel made entirely of heartwood?"

"No, venerable sir."

"In the same way, in whomever mindfulness immersed in the body is developed, is pursued, Mara gains no entry, Mara gains no foothold.

"Now, suppose that there were a wet, sappy piece of timber, and a man were to come along with an upper fire-stick, thinking, 'I'll light a fire. I'll produce heat.' What do you think—would he be able to light a fire and produce heat by rubbing the upper fire-stick in the wet, sappy piece of timber?"

"No, venerable sir."

"In the same way, in whomever mindfulness immersed in the body is developed, is pursued, Mara gains no entry, Mara gains no foothold.

"Now, suppose that there were a water-pot set on a stand, full of water up to the brim so that crows could drink out of it, and a man were to come along carrying a load of water. What do you think—would he get a place to put his water?"

"No, lord."

"In the same way, in whomever mindfulness immersed in the body is developed, is pursued, Mara gains no entry, Mara gains no foothold.

AN OPENING TO THE HIGHER KNOWLEDGES

"When anyone has developed & pursued mindfulness immersed in the body, then whichever of the six higher knowledges he turns his mind to know & realize, he can witness them for himself whenever there is an opening.

"Suppose that there were a water jar, set on a stand, brimful of water so that a crow could drink from it. If a strong man were to tip it in any way at all, would water spill out?"

"Yes, lord."

"In the same way, when anyone has developed & pursued mindfulness immersed in the body, then whichever of the six higher knowledges he turns his mind to know & realize, he can witness them for himself whenever there is an opening.

"Suppose there were a rectangular water tank—set on level ground, bounded by dikes—brimful of water so that a crow could drink from it. If a strong man were to loosen the dikes anywhere at all, would water spill out?"

"Yes, lord."

"In the same way, when anyone has developed & pursued mindfulness immersed in the body, then whichever of the six higher knowledges he turns his mind to know & realize, he can witness them for himself whenever there is an opening.

"Suppose there were a chariot on level ground at four crossroads, harnessed to thoroughbreds, waiting with whips lying ready, so that a skilled driver, a trainer of tamable horses, might mount and—taking the reins with his left hand and the whip with his right—drive out & back, to whatever place & by whichever road he liked; in the same way, when anyone has developed & pursued mindfulness immersed in the body, then whichever of the six higher knowledges he turns his mind to know & realize, he can witness them for himself whenever there is an opening.

TEN BENEFITS

"Monks, for one in whom mindfulness immersed in the body is cultivated, developed, pursued, given a means of transport, given a grounding, steadied, consolidated, & well-undertaken, ten benefits can be expected. Which ten?

"[1] He conquers displeasure & delight, and displeasure does not conquer him. He remains victorious over any displeasure that has arisen.

"[2] He conquers fear & dread, and fear & dread to not conquer him. He remains victorious over any fear & dread that have arisen.

"[3] He is resistant to cold, heat, hunger, thirst, the touch of gadflies & mosquitoes, wind & sun & creeping things; to abusive, hurtful language; he is the sort that can endure bodily feelings that, when they arise, are painful, sharp, stabbing, fierce, distasteful, disagreeable, deadly.

"[4] He can attain at will, without trouble or difficulty, the four jhanas—heightened mental states providing a pleasant abiding in the here & now.

"[5] He wields manifold supranormal powers. Having been one he becomes many; having been many he becomes one. He appears. He vanishes. He goes unimpeded through walls, ramparts, & mountains as if through space. He dives in & out of the earth as if it were water. He walks on water without sinking as if it were dry land. Sitting crosslegged he flies through the air like a winged bird. With his hand he touches & strokes even the sun & moon, so mighty & powerful. He exercises influence with his body even as far as the Brahma worlds.

"[6] He hears—by means of the divine ear-element, purified & surpassing the human—both kinds of sounds: divine & human, whether near or far.

"[7] He knows the awareness of other beings, other individuals, having encompassed it with his own awareness. He discerns a mind with passion as a mind with passion, and a mind without passion as a mind without passion. He discerns a mind with aversion as a mind with aversion, and a mind without aversion as a mind without aversion. He discerns a mind with delusion as a mind with delusion, and a mind without delusion as a mind without delusion. He discerns a restricted mind as a restricted mind, and a scattered mind as a scattered mind. He discerns an enlarged mind as an enlarged mind, and an unenlarged mind as an unenlarged mind. He discerns an excelled mind [one that is not at the most excellent level] as an excelled mind, and an unexcelled mind as an unexcelled mind. He discerns a concentrated mind as a concentrated mind, and an unconcentrated mind as an unconcentrated mind. He discerns a released mind as a released mind, and an unreleased mind as an unreleased mind.

"[8] He recollects his manifold past lives (lit: previous homes), i.e., one birth, two births, three births, four, five, ten, twenty, thirty, forty, fifty, one hundred, one thousand, one hundred thousand, many aeons of cosmic contraction, many aeons of cosmic expansion, many aeons of cosmic contraction & expansion, [recollecting], 'There I had such a name, belonged to such a clan, had such an appearance. Such was my food, such my experience of pleasure & pain, such the end of my life. Passing away from that state, I rearose there. There too I had such a name, belonged to such a clan, had such an appearance. Such was my food, such my experience of pleasure & pain, such the end of my life. Passing away from that state, I re-arose here.' Thus he remembers his manifold past lives in their modes & details.

"[9] He sees—by means of the divine eye, purified & surpassing the human—beings passing away & re-appearing, and he discerns how they are inferior & superior, beautiful & ugly, fortunate & unfortunate in accordance with their kamma: 'These beings—who were endowed with bad conduct of body, speech, & mind, who reviled the noble ones, held wrong views and undertook actions under the influence of wrong views—with the break-up of the body, after death, have re-appeared in the plane of deprivation, the bad destination, the lower realms, in hell. But these beings—who were endowed with good conduct of body, speech, & mind, who did not revile the noble ones, who held right views and undertook actions under the influence of right views—with the break-up of the body, after death, have re-appeared in the good destinations, in the heavenly world.' Thus—by means of the divine eye, purified & surpassing the human—he sees beings passing away & re-appearing, and he discerns how they are inferior & superior, beautiful & ugly, fortunate & unfortunate in accordance with their kamma.

"[10] Through the ending of the mental fermentations, he remains in the fermentation-free awareness-release & discernment-release, having known and made them manifest for himself right in the here & now.

"Monks, for one in whom mindfulness immersed in the body is cultivated, developed, pursued, given a means of transport, given a grounding, steadied, consolidated, & well-undertaken, these ten benefits can be expected."

That is what the Blessed One said. Gratified, the monks delighted in the Blessed One's words.

—MN 119

MINDFULNESS OF IN-&-OUT BREATHING

"Now how is mindfulness of in-&-out breathing developed & pursued so as to bring the four frames of reference to their culmination?

"There is the case where a monk, having gone to the wilderness, to the shade of a tree, or to an empty building, sits down folding his legs crosswise, holding his body erect, and setting mindfulness to the fore.[1] Always mindful, he breathes in; mindful he breathes out.

"[1] Breathing in long, he discerns that he is breathing in long; or breathing out long, he discerns that he is breathing out long. [2] Or breathing in short, he discerns that he is breathing in short; or breathing out short, he discerns that he is breathing out short. [3] He trains himself to breathe in sensitive to the entire body,[2] and to breathe out sensitive to the entire body. [4] He trains himself to breathe in calming bodily fabrication,[3] and to breathe out calming the bodily fabrication.

"[5] He trains himself to breathe in sensitive to rapture, and to breathe out sensitive to rapture. [6] He trains himself to breathe in sensitive to pleasure, and to breathe out sensitive to pleasure. [7] He trains himself to breathe in sensitive to mental fabrication,[4] and to breathe out sensitive to mental fabrication. [8] He trains himself to breathe in calming mental fabrication, and to breathe out calming mental fabrication.

"[9] He trains himself to breathe in sensitive to the mind, and to breathe out sensitive to the mind. [10] He trains himself to breathe in satisfying the mind, and to breathe out satisfying the mind. [11] He trains himself to breathe in steadying the mind, and to breathe out steadying the mind. [12] He trains himself to breathe in releasing the mind, and to breathe out releasing the mind.[5]

"[13] He trains himself to breathe in focusing on inconstancy, and to breathe out focusing on inconstancy. [14] He trains himself to breathe in focusing on dispassion [literally, fading], and to breathe out focusing on dispassion. [15] He trains himself to breathe in focusing on cessation, and to breathe out focusing on cessation. [16] He trains himself to breathe in focusing on relinquishment, and to breathe out focusing on relinquishment.

THE FOUR FRAMES OF REFERENCE

"[1] Now, on whatever occasion a monk breathing in long discerns that he is breathing in long; or breathing out long, discerns that he is breathing out long; or breathing in short, discerns that he is breathing in short; or breathing out short, discerns that he is breathing out short; trains himself to breathe in...&...out sensitive to the entire body; trains himself to breathe in...&...out calming bodily fabrication: On that occasion the monk remains focused on the *body* in & of itself—ardent, alert, & mindful—subduing greed & distress with reference to the world. I tell you, monks, that this—the in-&-out breath—is classed as a body among bodies, which is why the monk on that occasion remains focused on the body in & of itself—ardent, alert, & mindful—putting aside greed & distress with reference to the world.

"[2] On whatever occasion a monk trains himself to breathe in...&...out sensitive to rapture; trains himself to breathe in...&...out sensitive to pleasure; trains himself to breathe in...&...out sensitive to mental fabrication; trains himself to breathe in...&...out calming mental fabrication: On that occasion the monk remains focused on *feelings* in & of themselves—ardent, alert, & mindful—subduing greed & distress with reference to the world. I tell you, monks, that this—close attention to in-&-out breaths—is classed as a feeling among feelings,[6] which is why the monk on that occasion remains focused on feelings in & of themselves—

ardent, alert, & mindful—putting aside greed & distress with reference to the world.

"[3] On whatever occasion a monk trains himself to breathe in...&...out sensitive to the mind; trains himself to breathe in...&...out satisfying the mind; trains himself to breathe in...&...out steadying the mind; trains himself to breathe in...&...out releasing the mind: On that occasion the monk remains focused on the *mind* in & of itself—ardent, alert, & mindful—subduing greed & distress with reference to the world. I don't say that there is mindfulness of in-&-out breathing in one of confused mindfulness and no alertness, which is why the monk on that occasion remains focused on the mind in & of itself—ardent, alert, & mindful—putting aside greed & distress with reference to the world.

"[4] On whatever occasion a monk trains himself to breathe in...&...out focusing on inconstancy; trains himself to breathe in...&...out focusing on dispassion; trains himself to breathe in...&...out focusing on cessation; trains himself to breathe in...&...out focusing on relinquishment: On that occasion the monk remains focused on *mental qualities* in & of themselves—ardent, alert, & mindful—subduing greed & distress with reference to the world. He who sees clearly with discernment the abandoning of greed & distress is one who oversees with equanimity, which is why the monk on that occasion remains focused on mental qualities in & of themselves—ardent, alert, & mindful—putting aside greed & distress with reference to the world.

"This is how mindfulness of in-&-out breathing is developed & pursued so as to bring the four frames of reference to their culmination.

NOTES

1. To the fore *(parimukhaṁ):* The Abhidhamma takes an etymological approach to this term, defining it as around *(pari-)* the mouth *(mukhaṁ).* In the Vinaya, however, it is used in a context (Cv.V.27.4) where it undoubtedly means

the front of the chest. There is also the possibility that the term could be used idiomatically as "to the front," which is how I have translated it here.

2. The commentaries insist that "body" here means the breath, but this is unlikely in this context, for the next step—without further explanation—refers to the breath as "bodily fabrication." If the Buddha were using two different terms to refer to the breath in such close proximity, he would have been careful to signal that he was redefining his terms (as he does below, when explaining that the first four steps in breath meditation correspond to the practice of focusing on the body in and of itself as a frame of reference). The step of breathing in and out sensitive to the entire body relates to the many similes in the suttas depicting jhana as a state of whole-body awareness (see MN 119).

3. "In-&-out breaths are bodily; these are things tied up with the body. That's why in-&-out breaths are bodily fabrications."—MN 44.

4. "Perceptions & feelings are mental; these are things tied up with the mind. That's why perceptions & feelings are mental fabrications."—MN 44.

5. AN IX.34 shows how the mind, step by step, is temporarily released from burdensome mental states of greater and greater refinement as it advances through the stages of jhana.

6. As this shows, a meditator focusing on feelings in themselves as a frame of reference should not abandon the breath as the basis for his/her concentration.

—MN 118

III. The Advantages

of

Mindfulness Immersed in the Body

Khitaka:

How light my body!
Touched by abundant
rapture & bliss,
—like a cotton tuft
borne on the breeze—
it seems to be floating
—my body!

—*Thag I.104*

Ananda: "Lord, does the Blessed One have direct experience of going to the Brahma world by means of supranormal power with a mind-made body?"

The Buddha: "Yes, Ananda....'

Ananda: "But does the Blessed One also have direct experience of going to the Brahma world by means of supranormal power with this very physical body, composed of the four great elements?"

The Buddha: "Yes...."

Ananda: "It's awesome, lord, and amazing that the Blessed One should have direct experience of going to the Brahma world by means of supranormal power with a mind-made body, and of going to the Brahma world by means of supranormal power with this very physical body, composed of the four great elements."

The Buddha: "Tathagatas are both awesome, Ananda, and endowed with awesome qualities. They are both amazing and endowed with amazing qualities. Whenever the Tathagata merges his body with his mind and his mind with his body, and remains having alighted on the perception of ease and buoyancy with regard to the body, then his body becomes lighter, more pliant, more malleable, & more radiant.

"Just as when an iron ball heated all day becomes lighter, more pliant, more malleable, & more radiant; in the same way, whenever the Tathagata merges his body with his mind and his mind with his body, and remains having alighted on the perception of ease and buoyancy with regard to the body, then his body becomes lighter, more pliant, more malleable, & more radiant.

"Now, whenever the Tathagata merges his body with his mind and his mind with his body, and remains having alighted on the perception of ease and buoyancy with regard to the body, then his body rises effortlessly from the earth up into the sky. He then experiences manifold supra-normal powers. Having been one he becomes many; having been many he becomes one. He appears. He vanishes. He goes unimpeded through walls, ramparts, & mountains as if through space. He dives in & out of the earth as if it were water. He walks on water without sink-ing as if it were dry land. Sitting crosslegged he flies through the air like a winged bird. With his hand he touches & strokes even the sun & moon, so mighty & powerful. He exercises influence with his body even as far as the Brahma worlds.

"Just as a tuft of cotton seed or a ball of thistle down, lightly wafted by the wind, rises effortlessly from the earth up into the sky, in the same way, whenever the Tathagata concentrates his body in his mind & his mind in his body, and remains having alighted on the perception of ease and buoyancy, then his body rises effortlessly from the earth up into the sky. He then experiences manifold supranormal powers...even as far as the Brahma worlds."

—*SN LI.22*

Simply talking a lot
doesn't maintain the Dhamma.
Whoever
—although he's heard next to nothing—
sees Dhamma through his body,
is not heedless of Dhamma:
he's one who maintains the Dhamma.

—*Dhp 259*

They awaken, always wide awake:
Gotama's disciples
whose mindfulness, both day & night,
is constantly immersed
in the body.

—*Dhp 299*

"Once a hawk suddenly swooped down on a quail and seized it. Then the quail, as it was being carried off by the hawk, lamented, 'O, just my bad luck and lack of merit that I was wandering out of my proper range and into the territory of others! If only I had kept to my proper range today, to my own ancestral territory, this hawk would have been no match for me in battle.'

"'But what is your proper range?' the hawk asked. 'What is your own ancestral territory?'

"'A newly plowed field with clumps of earth all turned up.'

"So the hawk, without bragging about its own strength, without mentioning its own strength, let go of the quail. 'Go, quail, but even when you have gone there you won't escape me.'

"Then the quail, having gone to a newly plowed field with clumps of earth all turned up and climbing up on top of a large clump of earth, stood taunting the hawk, 'Now come and get me, you hawk! Now come and get me, you hawk!'

"So the hawk, without bragging about its own strength, without mentioning its own strength, folded its two wings and suddenly swooped down toward the quail. When the quail knew, 'The hawk is coming at me full speed,' it slipped behind the clump of earth, and right there the hawk shattered its breast.

"This is what happens to anyone who wanders into what is not his proper range and is the territory of others.

"For this reason, you should not wander into what is not your proper range and is the territory of others. In one who wanders into what is not his proper range and is the territory of others, Mara gains an opening, Mara gains a foothold. And what, for a monk, is not his proper range and is the territory of others? The five strands of sensuality. Which five? Forms cognizable by the eye—agreeable, pleasing, charming, endearing, fostering desire, enticing. Sounds cognizable by the ear...Smells cognizable by the nose...Tastes cognizable by the tongue...Tactile sensations cognizable by the body—agreeable, pleasing, charming, endearing, fostering desire, enticing. These, for a monk, are not his proper range and are the territory of others.

"Wander, monks, in what is your proper range, your own ancestral territory. In one who wanders in what is his proper range, his own ancestral territory, Mara gains no opening, Mara gains no foothold. And what, for a monk, is his proper range, his own ancestral territory? The four frames of reference. Which four? There is the case where a monk remains focused on the body in & of itself—ardent, alert, & mindful—putting aside greed & distress with reference to the world. He remains focused on feelings in & of themselves ... mind in & of itself ... mental qualities in & of themselves—ardent, alert, & mindful—putting aside greed & distress with reference to the world. This, for a monk, is his proper range, his own ancestral territory."

—*SN XLVII.6*

"There are in the Himalayas, the king of mountains, difficult, uneven areas where neither monkeys nor human beings wander. There are difficult, uneven areas where monkeys wander, but not human beings. There are level stretches of land, delightful, where both monkeys and human beings wander. In such spots hunters set a tar trap in the monkeys' tracks, in order to catch some monkeys. Those monkeys who are not foolish or careless by nature, when they see the tar trap, will keep their distance. But any monkey who is foolish & careless by nature comes up to the tar trap and grabs it with its paw, which then gets stuck there. Thinking, 'I'll free my paw,' he grabs it with his other paw. That too gets stuck. Thinking, 'I'll free both of my paws,' he grabs it with his foot. That too gets stuck. Thinking, 'I'll free both of my paws and my foot,' he grabs it with his other foot. That too gets stuck. Thinking, 'I'll free both of my paws and my feet as well,' he grabs it with his mouth. That too gets stuck. So the monkey, snared in five ways, lies there whimpering, having fallen on misfortune, fallen on ruin, a prey to whatever the hunter wants to do with him. Then the hunter, without releasing the monkey, skewers him right there, picks him up, and goes off as he likes.

"This is what happens to anyone who wanders into what is not his proper range and is the territory of others. For this reason, you should not wander into what is not your proper range and is the territory of others...."

—*SN XLVII.7*

"There is the case where a monk, seeing a form with the eye, is obsessed with pleasing forms, is repelled by unpleasing forms, and remains with body-mindfulness unestablished, with limited awareness. He does not discern, as it actually is present, the release of awareness, the release of discernment where any evil, unskillful mental qualities that have arisen utterly cease without remainder. (Similarly with ear, nose, tongue, body, & intellect.)

"Just as if a person, catching six animals of different ranges, of different habitats, were to bind them with a strong rope. Catching a snake, he would bind it with a strong rope. Catching a crocodile...a bird...a dog...a hyena... a monkey, he would bind it with a strong rope. Binding them all with a strong rope, and tying a knot in the middle, he would set chase to them.

"Then those six animals, of different ranges, of different habitats, would each pull toward its own range & habitat. The snake would pull, thinking, 'I'll go into the anthill.' The crocodile would pull, thinking, 'I'll go into the water.' The bird would pull, thinking, 'I'll fly up into the air.' The dog would pull, thinking, 'I'll go into the village.' The hyena would pull, thinking, 'I'll go into the charnel ground.' The monkey would pull, thinking, 'I'll go into the forest.' And when these six animals became internally exhausted, they would submit, they would surrender, they would come under the sway of whichever among them was the strongest. In the same way, when a monk whose mindfulness immersed in the body is undeveloped & unpursued, the eye pulls toward pleasing forms, while unpleasing forms are repellent. The ear pulls toward pleasing sounds...the nose pulls toward pleasing smells...the tongue pulls toward pleasing tastes...the body pulls toward pleasing tactile sensations...the intellect pulls toward pleasing ideas, while unpleasing ideas are repellent. This, monks, is lack of restraint.

"And what is restraint? There is the case where a monk, seeing a form with the eye, is not obsessed with pleasing forms, is not repelled by unpleasing forms, and remains with body-mindfulness established, with immeasurable awareness. He discerns, as it actually is present, the release of awareness, the release of discernment where all evil, unskillful mental qualities that have arisen utterly cease without remainder. (Similarly with ear, nose, tongue, body, & intellect.)

"Just as if a person, catching six animals of different ranges, of different habitats, were to bind them with a strong rope...and tether them to a strong post or stake. Then those six animals, of different ranges, of different habitats, would each pull toward its own range & habitat....And when these six animals became internally exhausted, they would stand, sit, or lie down right there next to the post or stake. In the same way, when a monk whose mindfulness immersed in the body is developed & pursued, the eye does not pull toward pleasing forms, and unpleasing forms are not repellent. The ear does not pull toward pleasing sounds...the nose does not pull toward pleasing smells...the tongue does not pull toward pleasing tastes...the body does not pull toward pleasing tactile sensations...the intellect does not pull toward pleasing ideas, and unpleasing ideas are not repellent. This, monks, is restraint.

"The 'strong post or stake' is a term for mindfulness immersed in the body.

Thus you should train yourselves: 'We will develop mindfulness immersed in the body. We will pursue it, give it a means of transport, give it a grounding. We will steady it, consolidate it, and set about it properly.' That's how you should train yourselves."

—SN XXXV.206

"Suppose, monks, that a large crowd of people comes thronging together, saying, 'The beauty queen! The beauty queen!' And suppose that the beauty queen is highly accomplished at singing & dancing, so that an even greater crowd comes thronging, saying, 'The beauty queen is singing! The beauty queen is dancing!' Then a man comes along, desiring life & shrinking from death, desiring pleasure & abhorring pain. They say to him, 'Now look here, mister. You must take this bowl filled to the brim with oil and carry it on your head in between the great crowd & the beauty queen. A man with a raised sword will follow right behind you, and wherever you spill even a drop of oil, right there will he cut off your head.' Now what do you think, monks: Will that man, not paying attention to the bowl of oil, let himself get distracted outside?"

"No, lord."

"I have given you this parable to convey a meaning. The meaning is this: The bowl filled to the brim with oil stands for mindfulness immersed in the body. Thus you should train yourselves: 'We will develop mindfulness immersed in the body. We will pursue it, give it a means of transport, give it a grounding. We will steady it, consolidate it, and set about it properly.' That's how you should train yourselves."

—*SN XLVII.20*

With mindfulness immersed in the body
well established,
restrained with respect to the six
media of contact,
always concentrated, the monk
can know Unbinding for himself.

—*Ud.III.5*

> Knowing this body
> is like foam,
> realizing its nature
>   —a mirage—
> cutting out
> the blossoms of Mara,
> you go where the King of Death
>   can't see.

—*Dhp 46*

"Whoever pervades the great ocean with his awareness encompasses whatever rivulets flow down into the ocean. In the same way, whoever develops & pursues mindfulness immersed in the body encompasses whatever skillful qualities are on the side of clear knowing."

"When one thing is practiced & pursued, the body is calmed, the mind is calmed, thinking & evaluating are stilled, and all qualities on the side of clear knowing go to the culmination of their development. Which one thing? Mindfulness immersed in the body."

"When one thing is practiced & pursued, ignorance is abandoned, clear knowing arises, the conceit 'I am' is abandoned, latent tendencies are uprooted, fetters are abandoned. Which one thing? Mindfulness immersed in the body."

"Those who do not taste mindfulness of the body do not taste the Deathless. Those who taste mindfulness of the body taste the Deathless."

"Those who are heedless of mindfulness of the body are heedless of the Deathless."

"Those who comprehend mindfulness of the body comprehend the Deathless."

—*AN I.225, 227, 230, 235, 239, 245*

IV. The Disadvantages
of Attachment to the Body

All too soon, this body
will lie on the ground
cast off,
bereft of consciousness,
like a useless scrap
of wood.

—*Dhp 41*

"The body is aflame. Tactile sensations are aflame. Bodily consciousness is aflame. Bodily contact is aflame. And whatever there is that arises in dependence on bodily contact—experienced as pleasure, pain or neither-pleasure-nor-pain—that too is aflame. Aflame with what? Aflame with the fire of passion, the fire of aversion, the fire of delusion. Aflame, I tell you, with birth, aging & death, with sorrows, lamentations, pains, distresses, & despairs....

"Seeing thus, the instructed disciple of the noble ones grows disenchanted with the body, disenchanted with tactile sensations, disenchanted with bodily consciousness, disenchanted with bodily contact. And whatever there is that arises in dependence on bodily contact, experienced as pleasure, pain or neither-pleasure-nor-pain: With that, too, he grows disenchanted.

"Disenchanted, he becomes dispassionate. Through dispassion, he is fully released. With full release, there is the knowledge, 'Fully released.' He discerns that 'Birth is depleted, the holy life fulfilled, the task done. There is nothing further for this world.'"

—*SN XXXV.28*

Then Janussonin the brahman went to the Blessed One and, on arrival, exchanged courteous greetings with him. After an exchange of friendly greetings & courtesies, he sat to one side. As he was sitting there he said to the Blessed One: "I am of the view & opinion that there is no one who, subject to death, is not afraid or in terror of death."

[The Blessed One said:] "Brahman, there are those who, subject to death, are afraid & in terror of death. And there are those who, subject to death, are not afraid or in terror of death.

"And who is the person who, subject to death, is afraid & in terror of death? There is the case of the person who has not abandoned passion, desire, fondness, thirst, fever, & craving for sensuality. Then he comes down with a serious disease. As he comes down with a serious disease, the thought occurs to him, 'O, those beloved sensual pleasures will be taken from me, and I will be taken from them!' He grieves & is tormented, weeps, beats his breast, & grows delirious. This is a person who, subject to death, is afraid & in terror of death.

"Then there is the case of the person who has not abandoned passion, desire, fondness, thirst, fever, & craving for the body. Then he comes down with a serious disease. As he comes down with a serious disease, the thought occurs to him, 'O, my beloved body will be taken from me, and I will be taken from my body!' He grieves & is tormented, weeps, beats his breast, & grows delirious. This, too, is a person who, subject to death, is afraid & in terror of death.

"Then there is the case of the person who has not done what is good, has not done what is skillful, has not given protection to those in fear, and instead has done what is evil, savage, & cruel. Then he comes down with a serious disease. As he comes down with a serious disease, the thought occurs to him, 'I have not done what is good, have not done what is skillful, have not given protection to those in fear, and instead have done what is evil, savage, & cruel. To the extent that there is a destination for those who have not done what is good, have not done what is skillful, have not given protection to those in fear, and instead have done what is evil, savage, & cruel, that's where I'm headed after death.' He grieves & is tormented, weeps, beats his breast, & grows delirious. This, too, is a person who, subject to death, is afraid & in terror of death.

"Then there is the case of the person in doubt & perplexity, who has not arrived at certainty with regard to the True Dhamma. Then he comes down with a serious disease. As he comes down with a serious disease, the thought occurs to him, 'How doubtful & perplexed I am! I have not arrived at any certainty with regard to the True Dhamma!' He grieves & is tormented, weeps, beats his breast, & grows delirious. This, too, is a person who, subject to death, is afraid & in terror of death.

"These, brahman, are four people who, subject to death, are afraid & in terror of death.

"And who is the person who, subject to death, is not afraid or in terror of death?

"There is the case of the person who has abandoned passion, desire, fondness, thirst, fever, & craving for sensuality. Then he comes down with a serious disease. As he comes down with a serious disease, the thought doesn't occur to him, 'O, those beloved sensual pleasures will be taken from me, and I will be taken from them!' He doesn't grieve, isn't tormented; doesn't weep, beat his breast, or grow delirious. This is a person who, subject to death, is not afraid or in terror of death.

"Then there is the case of the person who has abandoned passion, desire, fondness, thirst, fever, & craving for the body. Then he comes down with a serious disease. As he comes down with a serious disease, the thought doesn't occur to him, 'O, my beloved body will be taken from me, and I will be taken from my body!' He doesn't grieve, isn't tormented; doesn't weep, beat his breast, or grow delirious. This, too, is a person who, subject to death, is not afraid or in terror of death.

"Then there is the case of the person who has done what is good, has done what is skillful, has given protection to those in fear, and has not done what is evil, savage, or cruel. Then he comes down with a serious disease. As he comes down with a serious disease, the thought occurs to him, 'I have done what is good, have done what is skillful, have given protection to those in fear, and I have not done what is evil, savage, or cruel. To the extent that there is a destination for those who have done what is good, what is skillful, have given protection to those in fear, and have not done what is evil, savage, or cruel, that's where I'm headed after death.' He doesn't grieve, isn't tormented; doesn't weep, beat his breast, or grow delirious. This, too, is a person who, subject to death, is not afraid or in terror of death.

"Then there is the case of the person who has no doubt or perplexity, who has arrived at certainty with regard to the True Dhamma. Then he comes down with a serious disease. As he comes down with a serious disease, the thought occurs to him, 'I have no doubt or perplexity. I have arrived at certainty with regard to the True Dhamma.' He doesn't grieve, isn't tormented; doesn't weep, beat his breast, or grow delirious. This, too, is a person who, subject to death, is not afraid or in terror of death.

"These, brahman, are four people who, subject to death, are not afraid or in terror of death."

[When this was said, Janussonin the brahman said to the Blessed One:] "Magnificent, Master Gotama! Magnificent! Just as if he were to place upright what was overturned, to reveal what was hidden, to show the way to one who was lost, or to carry a lamp into the dark so that those with eyes could see forms, in the same way has Master Gotama— through many lines of reasoning—made the Dhamma clear. I go to Master Gotama for refuge, to the Dhamma, and to the Sangha of monks. May Master Gotama remember me as a lay follower who has gone to him for refuge, from this day forward, for life."

—AN IV.184

"And what is the perception of drawbacks? There is the case where a monk—having gone to the wilderness, to the foot of a tree, or to an empty dwelling—reflects thus: 'This body has many pains, many drawbacks. In this body many kinds of disease arise, such as: seeing-diseases, hearing-diseases, nose-diseases, tongue-diseases, body-diseases, head-diseases, ear-diseases, mouth-diseases, teeth-diseases, cough, asthma, catarrh, fever, aging, stomach-ache, fainting, dysentery, grippe, cholera, leprosy, boils, ringworm, tuberculosis, epilepsy, skin-diseases, itch, scab, psoriasis, scabies, jaundice, diabetes, hemorrhoids, fistulas, ulcers; diseases arising from bile, from phlegm, from the wind-property, from combinations of bodily humors, from changes in the weather, from uneven care of the body, from attacks, from the result of kamma; cold, heat, hunger, thirst, defecation, urination.' Thus he remains focused on drawbacks with regard to this body. This is called the perception of drawbacks."

—AN X.60

"I will teach you a Dhamma discourse on bondage & lack
of bondage. Listen & pay close attention. I will speak."
"Yes, lord," the monks responded.

The Blessed One said: "A woman attends inwardly to
her feminine faculties, her feminine gestures, her feminine
manners, feminine poise, feminine desires, feminine voice,
feminine charms. She is excited by that, delighted by that.
Being excited & delighted by that, she attends outwardly to
masculine faculties, masculine gestures, masculine manners,
masculine poise, masculine desires, masculine voices, masculine charms. She is excited by that, delighted by that. Being
excited & delighted by that, she wants to be bonded to what
is outside her, wants whatever pleasure & happiness that
arise based on that bond. Delighting, caught up in her femininity, a woman goes into bondage with reference to men.
This is how a woman does not transcend her femininity.

"A man attends inwardly to his masculine faculties,
masculine gestures, masculine manners, masculine poise,
masculine desires, masculine voice, masculine charms. He
is excited by that, delighted by that. Being excited &
delighted by that, he attends outwardly to feminine faculties, feminine gestures, feminine manners, feminine poise,
feminine desires, feminine voices, feminine charms. He is
excited by that, delighted by that. Being excited &
delighted by that, he wants to be bonded to what is outside
him, wants whatever pleasure & happiness that arise based
on that bond. Delighting, caught up in his masculinity, a
man goes into bondage with reference to women. This is
how a man does not transcend his masculinity.

"And how is there lack of bondage? A woman does not
attend inwardly to her feminine faculties ... feminine
charms. She is not excited by that, not delighted by that ...
does not attend outwardly to masculine faculties ... masculine charms. She is not excited by that, not delighted by that
... does not want to be bonded to what is outside her, does

not want whatever pleasure & happiness that arise based on that bond. Not delighting, not caught up in her femininity, a woman does not go into bondage with reference to men. This is how a woman transcends her femininity.

"A man does not attend inwardly to his masculine faculties ... masculine charms. He is not excited by that, not delighted by that ... does not attend outwardly to feminine faculties ... feminine charms. He is not excited by that, not delighted by that ... does not want to be bonded to what is outside him, does not want whatever pleasure & happiness that arise based on that bond. Not delighting, not caught up in his masculinity, a man does not go into bondage with reference to women. This is how a man transcends his masculinity.

"This is how there is lack of bondage. And this is the Dhamma discourse on bondage & lack of bondage."

—AN VII.48

[Ven. Ananda teaches a nun:] "'This body comes into being through food. And yet it is by relying on food that food is to be abandoned.' Thus it was said. And in reference to what was it said? There is the case, sister, where a monk, considering it thoughtfully, takes food—not playfully, nor for intoxication, nor for putting on bulk, nor for beautification—but simply for the survival & continuance of this body, for ending its afflictions, for the support of the holy life, [thinking,] 'Thus will I destroy old feelings [of hunger] and not create new feelings [from overeating]. I will maintain myself, be blameless, & live in comfort.' Then, at a later time, he abandons food, having relied on food. 'This body, sister, comes into being through food. And yet it is by relying on food that food is to be abandoned.' Thus it was said, and in reference to this was it said.

"'This body comes into being through craving. And yet it is by relying on craving that craving is to be abandoned.' Thus it was said. And in reference to what was it said? There is the case, sister, where a monk hears, 'The monk named such-and-such, they say, through the ending of the fermentations, has entered & remains in the fermentation- & discernment-release, having known & realized them for himself in the here & now.' The thought occurs to him, 'I hope that I, too, will—through the ending of the fermentations—enter & remain in the fermentation-free awareness-release & discernment-release, having directly known & realized them for myself right in the here & now.' Then, at a later time, he abandons craving, having relied on craving. 'This body comes into being through craving. And yet it is by relying on craving that craving is to be abandoned.' Thus it was said. And in reference to this was it said.

"'This body comes into being through conceit. And yet it is by relying on conceit that conceit is to be abandoned.' Thus it was said. And in reference to what was it said? There is the case, sister, where a monk hears, 'The monk named such-and-such, they say, through the ending of the fermentations, has entered & remains in the fermentation-free awareness-release & discernment-release, having directly known & realized them for himself right in the here & now.' The thought occurs to him, 'The monk named such-&-such, they say, through the ending of the fermentations, has entered & remains in the fermentation-free awareness-release & discernment-release, having directly known & realized them for himself right in the here & now. Then why not me?' Then, at a later time, he abandons conceit, having relied on conceit. 'This body comes into being through conceit. And yet it is by relying on conceit that conceit is to be abandoned.' Thus it was said, and in reference to this was it said.

"This body comes into being through sexual intercourse. Sexual intercourse is to be abandoned. With regard to sexual intercourse, the Buddha declares the cutting off of the bridge."

—*AN IV.159*

Look at the beautified image,
a heap of festering wounds, shored up:
ill, but the object
            of many resolves,
where there is nothing
            lasting or sure.

Worn out is this body,
a nest of diseases, dissolving.
This putrid conglomeration
is bound to break up,
for life is hemmed in with death.

On seeing these bones
            discarded
like gourds in the fall,
            pigeon-gray:
                        what delight?

A city made of bones,
plastered over with flesh & blood,
whose hidden treasures are:
            pride & contempt,
            aging & death.

—*Dhp 147-150*

Whether walking, standing,
sitting, or lying down,
it flexes & stretches:
> this is the body's movement.
Joined together with tendons & bones,
plastered over with muscle & skin,
hidden by complexion,
> the body isn't seen
> for what it is:
filled with intestines, filled with stomach,
with the lump of the liver,
bladder, lungs, heart,
kidneys, spleen,
mucus, sweat, saliva, fat,
blood, synovial fluid, bile, & oil.
On top of that,
in nine streams,
filth is always flowing from it:
from the eyes : eye secretions,
from the ears : ear secretions,
from the nose : mucus,
from the mouth : now vomit,
> now phlegm,
> now bile.
from the body : beads of sweat.
And on top of that,
its hollow head is filled with brains.

The fool, beset by ignorance,
thinks it beautiful,
but when it lies dead—
> swollen, livid,
> cast away in a charnel ground—
even relatives don't care for it.
Dogs feed on it,
jackals, wolves, & worms.

Crows & vultures feed on it,
along with any other animals there.

Having heard the Awakened One's words,
the discerning monk
comprehends, for he sees it
        for what it is:
"As this is, so is that.
As that, so this."
Within & without,
he should let desire for the body
        fade away.
With desire & passion faded away,
the discerning monk arrives here:
        at the deathless,
        the calm,
        the undying state
        of Unbinding.

This two-footed, filthy, evil-smelling,
filled-with-various-carcasses,
oozing-out-here-&-there body:
Whoever would think,
on the basis of a body like this,
to exalt himself or disparage another:
        What is that
        if not blindness?

                                        —Sn I.11

"Monks, it's just as if there were a boil that had been building for many years with nine openings, nine un-lanced
heads. Whatever would ooze out from it would be an
uncleanliness oozing out, a stench oozing out, a disgust
oozing out. Whatever would be discharged from it would
be an uncleanliness discharging, a stench discharging, a
disgust discharging.

"'A boil,' monks, is another word for this body composed of the four properties, born of mother & father, fed on rice & porridge, subject to inconstancy, rubbing & massaging, breaking-up & disintegrating. It has nine openings, nine un-lanced heads. Whatever would ooze out from it would be an uncleanliness oozing out, a stench oozing out, a disgust oozing out. Whatever would be discharged from it would be an uncleanliness discharging, a stench discharging, a disgust discharging. For that reason, you should become disenchanted with this body."

—*AN IX.15*

Pingiya:

I'm old & weak,
my complexion dull.
I've blurry eyes
and trouble hearing,
but may I not perish deluded,
                              confused!
Teach me the Dhamma
so that I may know
the abandoning here
        of birth & aging.

The Buddha:

Seeing people suffering
on account of their bodies—
        heedless people are oppressed
        on account of their bodies—
then heedful, Pingiya,
let go of the body
        for the sake of no further becoming.

Pingiya:

In the four cardinal directions,
the four intermediate,
above & below
    —the ten directions—
there is nothing in the world
    unseen, unheard,
    unsensed, uncognized by you.
Teach me the Dhamma
so that I may know
the abandoning here
    of birth & aging.

The Buddha:

Seeing people,
    victims of craving—
    aflame, overwhelmed with aging—
then heedful, Pingiya,
let go of craving
    for the sake of no further becoming.

—Sn V.16

Manava:

On seeing an old person;
    &
a person in pain, diseased;
    &
a person dead, gone to life's end,
    I left
for the life gone forth,
    abandoning the sensuality
    that entices the heart.

—Thag I.73

All too soon, this body
will lie on the ground
      cast off,
bereft of consciousness,
like a useless scrap
      of wood.

—Dhp 41

Look at the beautified image,
a heap of festering wounds, shored up:
ill, but the object
      of many desires,
where there is nothing
      lasting or sure.

—Dhp 147

A city made of bones,
plastered over with flesh & blood,
whose hidden treasures are:
      pride & contempt,
      aging & death.

—Dhp 150

This unlistening man
matures like an ox.
His muscles develop,
his discernment   not.

—Dhp 152

    Kimbila:

As if sent by a curse,
it drops on us—
          aging.

The body seems   other,
though it's still the same one.
I'm still here
& have never been absent from it,
but I remember myself
as if somebody else's.

—Thag I.118

Mahakala:

This swarthy woman
[preparing a corpse for cremation]
        —crow-like, enormous—
breaking a thigh & then the other
        thigh,
breaking an arm & then the other
                arm,
cracking open the head,
        like a pot of curds,
she sits with them heaped up beside her.

Whoever, unknowing,
makes acquisitions
        —the fool—
returns over & over
to suffering & stress.
So, discerning,
don't make acquisitions.
        May I never lie
        with my head cracked open
                again.

—Thag II.16

Rajadata:

I, a monk,
gone to the charnel ground,

saw a woman cast away,
    discarded
there in the cemetery.

Though some were disgusted,
seeing her—dead, evil—
                lust
    appeared,
as if I were blind
    to the oozings.

In less time than it takes
for rice to cook,
I got out of that place.
Mindful, alert, I
sat down to one side.
Then apt attention arose in me,
the drawbacks appeared,
    disenchantment stood
    at an even keel:

With that, my heart was released.
See the Dhamma's true rightness!
The three knowledges
have been attained;
the Awakened One's bidding,
    done.

—Thag V.1

As Subha the nun was going through Jivaka's delightful mango grove, a libertine (a goldsmith's son) blocked her path, so she said to him:

'What wrong have I done you
that you stand in my way?
It's not proper, my friend,

that a man should touch
a woman gone forth.
I respect the Master's message,
the training pointed out by the one well-gone.
I am pure, without blemish:
        Why do you stand in my way?
You—your mind agitated, impassioned;
I—unagitated, unimpassioned,
with a mind entirely freed:
        Why do you stand in my way?'

'You are young & not bad-looking,
what need do you have for going forth?
Throw off your ochre robe—
        Come, let's delight in the flowering grove.
A sweetness they exude everywhere,
the towering trees with their pollen.
The beginning of spring is a pleasant season—
        Come, let's delight in the flowering grove.
The trees with their blossoming tips
moan, as it were, in the breeze:
What delight will you have
if you plunge into the grove alone?
Frequented by herds of wild beasts,
disturbed by elephants rutting & aroused:
you want to go
        unaccompanied
into the great, lonely, frightening grove?

Like a doll made of gold, you will go about,
like a goddess in the gardens of heaven.
With delicate, smooth Kasi fabrics,
you will shine, O beauty without compare.
I would gladly do your every bidding
if we were to dwell in the glade.

For there is no creature dearer to me
        than you, O nymph with the languid regard.
If you do as I ask, happy, come live in my house.
Dwelling in the calm of a palace,
        have women wait on you,
        wear delicate Kasi fabrics,
        adorn yourself with garlands & creams.
I will make you many & varied ornaments
        of gold, jewels, & pearls.
Climb onto a costly bed,
scented with sandalwood carvings,
with a well-washed coverlet, beautiful,
spread with a woolen quilt, brand new.

Like a blue lotus rising from the water
where no human beings dwell,
you will go to old age with your limbs unseen,
if you stay as you are in the holy life.'

'What do you assume of any essence,
here in this cemetery grower, filled with corpses,
this body destined to break up?
What do you see when you look at me,
        you who are out of your mind?'

        'Your eyes
are like those of a fawn,
like those of a sprite in the mountains.
Seeing your eyes, my sensual delight
        grows all the more.
Like tips they are, of blue lotuses,
in your golden face
        —spotless:
Seeing your eyes, my sensual delight
        grows all the more.
Even if you should go far away,

I will think only of your pure,
     long-lashed gaze,
for there is nothing dearer to me
than your eyes, O nymph with the languid regard.'

'You want to stray from the road,
you want the moon as a plaything,
you want to jump over Mount Sineru,
you who have designs on one born of the Buddha.
For there is nothing anywhere at all
in the cosmos with its gods,
that would be an object of passion for me.
I don't even know what that passion would be,
     for it's been killed, root & all, by the path.
Like embers from a pit—scattered,
like a bowl of poison—evaporated,
     I don't even see what that passion would be,
     for it's been killed, root & all, by the path.
Try to seduce one who hasn't reflected on this,
or who has not followed the Master's teaching.
But try it with this one who knows
     and you suffer.
For in the midst of praise & blame,
     pleasure & pain,
my mindfulness stands firm.
Knowing the unattractiveness
     of things compounded,
my mind cleaves to nothing at all.
I am a follower of the one well-gone,
riding the vehicle of the eightfold way:
My arrow removed, fermentation-free,
I delight, having gone to an empty dwelling.
For I have seen well-painted puppets,
hitched up with sticks & strings,
made to dance in various ways.

When the sticks & strings are removed,
thrown away, scattered, shredded,
smashed into pieces, not to be found,
     in what will the mind there make its home?
This body of mine, which is just like that,
when devoid of dhammas doesn't function.
When, devoid of dhammas, it doesn't function,
     in what will the mind there make its home?

Like a mural you've seen, painted on a wall,
smeared with yellow orpiment,
there your vision has been distorted,
meaningless your human perception.
Like an evaporated mirage,
like a tree of gold in a dream,
like a magic show in the midst of a crowd—
     you run blind after what is unreal.
Resembling a ball of sealing wax,
set in a hollow,
with a bubble in the middle
and bathed with tears,
eye secretions are born there too:
The parts of the eye
are rolled all together
in various ways.'

Plucking out her lovely eye,
with mind unattached
she felt no regret.

'Here, take this eye. It's yours.'

Straightaway she gave it to him.
Straightaway his passion faded right there,
and he begged her forgiveness.

'Be well, follower of the holy life.
          This sort of thing
          won't happen again.
Harming a person like you
is like embracing a blazing fire.
It's as if I have seized a poisonous snake.
So may you be well. Forgive me.'

And released from there, the nun
went to the excellent Buddha's presence.
When she saw the mark of his excellent merit,
          her eye became
          as it was before.

                              —*Thig XIV*

Ornamented, finely clothed
          garlanded, adorned,
her feet stained red with lac,
          she wore slippers:
                    a courtesan.
Stepping out of her slippers—
          her hands raised before me,
          palm-to-palm over her heart—
she softly, tenderly,
          in measured words
          spoke to me first:
"You are young, recluse.
          Heed my message:
Partake of human sensuality.
          I will give you luxury.
Truly I vow to you,
          I will tend to you as to a fire.
When we are old,
          both leaning on canes,

then we will both become contemplatives,
    winning the benefits of both worlds."

And seeing her before me—
    a courtesan, ornamented, finely clothed,
    hands palm-to-palm over her heart—
        like a snare of death laid out,
apt attention arose in me,
    the drawbacks appeared,
        disenchantment stood
        at an even keel:

With that, my heart was released.
See the Dhamma's true rightness!
The three knowledges
have been attained;
the Buddha's bidding,
    done.

                —*Thag VII.1*

    Kappa:

Full of the many clans of impurities,
the great manufacturer of excrement,
like a stagnant pool,
    a great tumor,
    great wound,
full of blood & lymph,
immersed in a cesspool,
trickling liquids,   the body
is oozing foulness—always.
Bound together with sixty sinews,
plastered with a stucco of muscle,
wrapped in a jacket of skin,
this foul body is of no worth at all.
Linked together with a chain of bones,
stitched together with tendon-threads,

it produces its various postures,
from being hitched up together.

Headed surely to death,
in the presence of the King of Mortality,
the man who learns to discard it right here,
   goes wherever he wants.

Covered with ignorance,
the body's tied down with a four-fold tie,[1]
   sunk in the floods,[2]
   caught in the net of obsessions,[3]
   conjoined with five hindrances,[4]
   given over to thought,
   accompanied with the root of craving,
   roofed with delusion's roofing.
That's how the body functions,
compelled by the compulsion of kamma,
   but its attainment ends
     in ruin.
   Its many becomings go
     to ruin.

These who hold to this body as *mine*
—blind fools, people run-of-the-mill—
fill the horrific cemetery,
taking on further becoming.
Those who stay uninvolved with this body
—as they would with a serpent
   smeared with dung—
disgorging the root of becoming,[5]
from lack of fermentation
   will be totally Unbound.

NOTES

1. The four-fold tie: greed, ill will, attachment to precepts & practice, and dogmatic obsession with views.
2. Floods: sensuality, becoming, views, and ignorance. See SN XLV.171. These are identical with the four yokes. See AN IV.10.
3. Obsessions: sensual psssion, resistance, views, uncertainty, conceit, passion for becoming, and ignorance. See AN VII.11-12.
4. Hindrances: sensual desire, ill will, sloth & torpor, restlessness & anxiety, and uncertainty. See DN 2 and SN XLVI.51.
5. The root of becoming: craving.

—Thag X.5

Ampabali:

Black was my hair
—the color of bees—
& curled at the tips;
  with age, it looked like coarse hemp.
The truth of the Truth-speaker's words
   doesn't change.

Fragrant, like a perfumed basket
filled with flowers: my coiffure.
  With age it smelled musty,
  like animal fur.
The truth of the Truth-speaker's words
   doesn't change.

Thick & lush, like a well-tended grove,
made splendid, the tips elaborate
with comb & pin.
  With age, it grew thin
  & bald here & there.

The truth of the Truth-speaker's words
        doesn't change.

Adorned with gold & delicate pins,
it was splendid, ornamented with braids.
        Now, with age,
        that head has gone bald.
The truth of the Truth-speaker's words
        doesn't change.

Curved, as if well-drawn by an artist,
my brows were once splendid.
        With age, they droop down in folds.
The truth of the Truth-speaker's words
        doesn't change.

Radiant, brilliant like jewels,
my eyes: elongated, black—deep black.
        With age, they're no longer splendid.
The truth of the Truth-speaker's words
        doesn't change.

Like a delicate peak, my nose
was splendid in the prime of my youth.
        With age, it's like a long pepper.
The truth of the Truth-speaker's words
        doesn't change.

Like bracelets—well-fashioned, well-finished—
my ears were once splendid.
        With age, they droop down in folds.
The truth of the Truth-speaker's words
        doesn't change.

Like plaintain buds in their color,
my teeth were once splendid.
        With age, they're broken & yellowed.
The truth of the Truth-speaker's words
        doesn't change.

Like that of a cuckoo in the dense jungle,
flitting through deep forest thickets:
sweet was the tone of my voice.
   With age, it cracks here & there.
The truth of the Truth-speaker's words
    doesn't change.

Smooth—like a conch shell well-polished—
my neck was once splendid.
   With age, it's broken down, bent.
The truth of the Truth-speaker's words
    doesn't change.

Like rounded door-bars—both of them—
my arms were once splendid.
   With age, they're like dried up patali trees.
The truth of the Truth-speaker's words
    doesn't change.

Adorned with gold & delicate rings,
my hands were once splendid.
   With age, they're like onions & tubers.
The truth of the Truth-speaker's words
    doesn't change.

Swelling, round, firm, & high,
both my breasts were once splendid.
   In the drought of old age, they dangle
   like empty old water bags.
The truth of the Truth-speaker's words
    doesn't change.

Like a sheet of gold, well-burnished,
my body was splendid.
   Now it's covered with very fine wrinkles.
The truth of the Truth-speaker's words
    doesn't change.

Smooth in their lines, like an elephant's trunk,
both my thighs were once splendid.
    With age, they're like knotted bamboo.
The truth of the Truth-speaker's words
    doesn't change.

Adorned with gold & delicate anklets,
my calves were once splendid.
    With age, they're like sesame sticks.
The truth of the Truth-speaker's words
    doesn't change.

As if they were stuffed with soft cotton,
both my feet were once splendid.
    With age, they're shriveled & cracked.
The truth of the Truth-speaker's words
    doesn't change.

Such was this physical heap,
now: decrepit, the home of pains, many pains.
    A house with its plaster all fallen off.
The truth of the Truth-speaker's words

    doesn't change.

        —*Thig XIII.1*

    Nanda:

"Sick, putrid, unclean:
look, Nanda, at this physical heap.
Through contemplation of the foul,
develop your mind,
make it one, well-centered.

    As this [your body], so that.
    As that, so this.
It gives off a foul stench,
the delight of fools."

Considering it thus,
untiring, both day & night,
I, with my own discernment
          dissecting it,
                    saw.

And as I, heedful,
          examined it aptly,
this body—as it actually is—
was seen inside & out.

Then was I disenchanted with the body
          & dispassionate within:
Heedful, detached,
          calmed was I.

                    Unbound.

                                        —*Thig V.4*

          Sona:

Ten children I bore
from this physical heap.
Then weak from that, aged,
I went to a nun.
She taught me the Dhamma:
          aggregates, sense spheres, & elements.
Hearing her Dhamma,
I cut off my hair & ordained.
Having purified the divine eye
while still a probationer,
I know my previous lives,
where I lived in the past.
I develop the theme-less meditation,
well-focused oneness.

I gain the liberation of immediacy—
from lack of clinging, unbound.

The five aggregates, comprehended,
stand like a tree with its root cut through.
  I spit on old age.
There is now no further becoming.

        —*Thig V.8*

V. Samatha / Vipassana

"These two qualities have a share in clear knowing. Which two? Tranquility *(samatha)* & insight *(vipassana)*.

"When tranquility is developed, what purpose does it serve? The mind is developed. And when the mind is developed, what purpose does it serve? Passion is abandoned.

"When insight is developed, what purpose does it serve? Discernment is developed. And when discernment is developed, what purpose does it serve? Ignorance is abandoned."

—AN II.29

"Suppose that there were a royal frontier fortress with strong ramparts, strong walls & arches, and six gates. In it would be a wise, competent, knowledgeable gatekeeper to keep out those he didn't know and to let in those he did. A swift pair of messengers, coming from the east, would say to the gatekeeper, 'Where, my good man, is the commander of this fortress?' He would say, 'There he is, sirs, sitting in the central square.' The swift pair of messengers, delivering their accurate report to the commander of the fortress, would then go back by the route by which they had come. Then a swift pair of messengers, coming from the west ... the north ... the south, would say to the gatekeeper, 'Where, my good man, is the commander of this fortress?' He would say, 'There he is, sirs, sitting in the central square.' The swift pair of messengers, delivering their accurate report to the commander of the fortress, would then go back by the route by which they had come.

"I have given you this simile to convey a message. The message is this: The fortress stands for this body—composed of four elements, born of mother & father, nourished with rice & barley gruel, subject to constant rubbing & abrasion, to breaking & falling apart. The six gates stand for the six internal sense media. The gatekeeper stands for mindfulness. The swift pair of messengers stands for tranquility *(samatha)* and insight *(vipassana)*. The commander of the fortress stands for consciousness. The central square stands for the four great elements: the earth-property, the liquid-property, the fire-property, & the wind-property. The accurate report stands for Unbinding *(nibbana)*. The route by which they had come stands for the noble eightfold path: right view, right resolve, right speech, right action, right livelihood, right effort, right mindfulness, right concentration."

—*SN XXXV.204*

On one occasion Ven. Ananda was staying in Kosambi, at Ghosita's monastery. There he addressed the monks, "Friends!"

"Yes, friend," the monks responded.

Ven. Ananda said: "Friends, whoever—monk or nun—declares the attainment of arahantship in my presence, they all do it by means of one or another of four paths. Which four?

"There is the case where a monk has developed insight preceded by tranquility. As he develops insight preceded by tranquility, the path is born. He follows that path, develops it, pursues it. As he follows the path, developing it & pursuing it—his fetters are abandoned, his obsessions destroyed.

"Then there is the case where a monk has developed tranquility preceded by insight. As he develops tranquility preceded by insight, the path is born. He follows that path, develops it, pursues it. As he follows the path, developing it & pursuing it—his fetters are abandoned, his obsessions destroyed.

"Then there is the case where a monk has developed tranquility in tandem with insight. As he develops tranquility in tandem with insight, the path is born. He follows that path, develops it, pursues it. As he follows the path, developing it & pursuing it—his fetters are abandoned, his obsessions destroyed.

"Then there is the case where a monk's mind has its restlessness concerning the Dhamma [Comm: the corruptions of insight] well under control. There comes a time when his mind grows steady inwardly, settles down, and becomes unified & concentrated. In him the path is born. He follows that path, develops it, pursues it. As he follows the path, developing it & pursuing it—his fetters are abandoned, his obsessions destroyed.

"Whoever—monk or nun—declares the attainment of arahantship in my presence, they all do it by means of one or another of these four paths."

—AN IV.170

"Monks, these four types of individuals are to be found existing in world. Which four?

"There is the case of the individual who has attained internal tranquility of awareness, but not insight into phenomena through heightened discernment. Then there is the case of the individual who has attained insight into phenomena through heightened discernment, but not internal tranquility of awareness. Then there is the case of the individual who has attained neither internal tranquility of awareness nor insight into phenomena through heightened discernment. And then there is the case of the individual who has attained both internal tranquility of awareness & insight into phenomena through heightened discernment.

"The individual who has attained internal tranquility of awareness, but not insight into phenomena through heightened discernment, should approach an individual who has attained insight into phenomena through heightened discernment and ask him: 'How should fabrications be regarded? How should they be investigated? How should they be seen with insight?' The other will answer in line with what he has seen & experienced: 'Fabrications should be regarded in this way. Fabrications should be investigated in this way. Fabrications should be seen in this way with insight.' Then eventually he [the first] will become one who has attained both internal tranquility of awareness & insight into phenomena through heightened discernment.

"As for the individual who has attained insight into phenomena through heightened discernment, but not internal tranquility of awareness, he should approach an individual who has attained internal tranquility of awareness... and ask him, 'How should the mind be steadied? How should it be made to settle down? How should it be unified? How should it be concentrated?' The other will answer in line with what he has seen & experienced: 'The mind should be steadied in this way. The mind should be made to settle down in this way. The mind should be unified in this way. The mind should be concentrated in this way.' Then eventually he [the first] will become one who has attained both internal tranquility of awareness & insight into phenomena through heightened discernment.

"As for the individual who has attained neither internal tranquility of awareness nor insight into phenomena through heightened discernment, he should approach an individual who has attained both internal tranquility of awareness & insight into phenomena through heightened discernment...and ask him, 'How should the mind be steadied? How should it be made to settle down? How should it be unified? How should it be concentrated? How should fabrications be regarded? How should they be investigated? How should they be seen with insight?' The other will answer in line with what he has seen & experienced: 'The mind should be steadied in this way. The mind should be made to settle down in this way. The mind should be unified in this way. The mind should be concentrated in this way. Fabrications should be regarded in this way. Fabrications should be investigated in this way. Fabrications should be seen in this way with insight.' Then eventually he [the first] will become one who has attained both internal tranquility of awareness & insight into phenomena through heightened discernment.

"As for the individual who has attained both internal tranquility of awareness & insight into phenomena through heightened discernment, his duty is to make an effort in establishing ('tuning') those very same skillful qualities to a higher degree for the ending of the (mental) fermentations.

"These are four types of individuals to be found existing in world."

—AN IV.94

"Not knowing, not seeing the body as it actually is present; not knowing, not seeing tactile sensations ... consciousness at the body... contact at the body as they actually are present; not knowing, not seeing whatever arises conditioned through contact at the body—experienced as pleasure, pain, or neither-pleasure-nor-pain—as it actually is present, one is infatuated with the body ... ideas ... consciousness at the body... contact at the body ... whatever arises conditioned by contact at the body and is experienced as pleasure, pain, or neither-pleasure-nor-pain.

"For him—infatuated, attached, confused, not remaining focused on their drawbacks—the five clinging-aggregates head toward future accumulation. The craving that makes for further becoming—accompanied by passion & delight, relishing now this & now that—grows within him. His bodily disturbances & mental disturbances grow. His bodily torments & mental torments grow. His bodily distresses & mental distresses grow. He is sensitive both to bodily stress & mental stress....

"However, knowing & seeing the body as it actually is present, knowing & seeing tactile sensations ... consciousness at the body... contact at the body as they actually are present, knowing & seeing whatever arises conditioned through contact at the body—experienced as pleasure, pain, or neither-pleasure-nor-pain—as it actually is present, one is not infatuated with the body ... tactile sensations ... consciousness at the body ... contact at the body ... whatever arises conditioned by contact at the body and is experienced as pleasure, pain, or neither-pleasure-nor-pain.

"For him—uninfatuated, unattached, unconfused, remaining focused on their drawbacks—the five clinging-aggregates head toward future diminution. The craving that makes for further becoming—accompanied by passion & delight, relishing now this & now that—is abandoned by him. His bodily disturbances & mental disturbances are abandoned. His bodily torments & mental torments are abandoned. His bodily distresses & mental distresses are abandoned. He is sensitive both to ease of body & ease of awareness.

"Any view belonging to one who has come to be like this is his right view. Any resolve, his right resolve. Any effort, his right effort. Any mindfulness, his right mindfulness. Any concentration, his right concentration: just as earlier his actions, speech, & livelihood were already well-purified. Thus for him, having thus developed the noble eightfold path, the four frames of reference go to the culmination of their development. The four right exertions ... the four bases of power ... the five faculties ... the five strengths ... the seven factors for Awakening go to the culmination of their development. [And] for him these two qualities occur in tandem: tranquility & insight.

"He comprehends through direct knowledge whatever qualities are to be comprehended through direct knowledge, abandons through direct knowledge whatever qualities are to be abandoned through direct knowledge, develops through direct knowledge whatever qualities are to be developed through direct knowledge, and realizes through direct knowledge whatever qualities are to be realized through direct knowledge.

"And what qualities are to be comprehended through direct knowledge? 'The five clinging-aggregates,' should be the reply. Which five? Form as a clinging-aggregate ... feeling ... perception ... fabrications ... consciousness as a clinging-aggregate. These are the qualities that are to be comprehended through direct knowledge.

"And what qualities are to be abandoned through direct knowledge? Ignorance & craving for becoming: these are the qualities that are to be abandoned through direct knowledge.

"And what qualities are to be developed through direct knowledge? Tranquility & insight: these are the qualities that are to be developed through direct knowledge.

"And what qualities are to be realized through direct knowledge? Clear knowing & release: these are the qualities that are to be realized through direct knowledge."

—*MN 149*

[Insight & tranquility as a prerequisite for jhana:] "If a monk would wish, 'May I attain—whenever I want, without strain, without difficulty—the four jhanas that are heightened mental states, pleasant abidings in the here-&-now,' then he should be one who brings the precepts to perfection, who is committed to mental tranquility, who does not neglect jhana, who is endowed with insight, and who frequents empty dwellings.

—*AN X.71*

VI. Mindfulness / Jhana

Visakha: "Now what is concentration, what qualities are its themes, what qualities are its requisites, and what is its development?"

Sister Dhammadinna: "Singleness of mind is concentration; the four frames of reference are its themes; the four right exertions are its requisites; and any cultivation, development, & pursuit of these qualities is its development."

—MN 44

[A certain monk:] "May the Blessed One teach me the Dhamma in brief! May the One Well-gone teach me the Dhamma in brief! It may well be that I will understand the Blessed One's words. It may well be that I will become an heir to the Blessed One's words."

[The Buddha:] "Then, monk, you should train yourself thus: 'My mind will be established inwardly, well-composed. No evil, unskillful qualities, once they have arisen, will remain consuming the mind.' That's how you should train yourself.

"Then you should train yourself thus: 'Good will, as my awareness-release, will be developed, pursued, given a means of transport, given a grounding, steadied, consolidated, & well-undertaken.' That's how you should train yourself. When you have developed this concentration in this way, you should develop this concentration with directed thought & evaluation, you should develop it with no directed thought & a modicum of evaluation, you should develop it with no directed thought & no evaluation, you should develop it accompanied by rapture ... not accompanied by rapture ... endowed with a sense of enjoyment; you should develop it endowed with equanimity.

"When this concentration is thus developed, thus well-developed by you, you should then train yourself thus: 'Compassion, as my awareness-release .... Appreciation, as my awareness-release .... Equanimity, as my awareness-release, will be developed, pursued, given a means of transport, given a grounding, steadied, consolidated, & well-undertaken.' That's how you should train yourself. When you have developed this concentration in this way, you should develop this concentration with directed thought & evaluation, you should develop it with no directed thought & a modicum of evaluation, you should develop it with no directed thought & no evaluation, you should develop it accompanied by rapture ... not accompanied by rapture ... endowed with a sense of enjoyment; you should develop it endowed with equanimity.

"When this concentration is thus developed, thus well-developed by you, you should then train yourself thus: 'I will remain focused on the body in & of itself—ardent, alert, & mindful—putting aside greed & distress with reference to the world.' That's how you should train yourself. When you have developed this concentration in this way, you should develop this concentration with directed thought & evaluation, you should develop it with no directed thought & a modicum of evaluation, you should develop it with no directed thought & no evaluation, you should develop it accompanied by rapture ... not accompanied by rapture ... endowed with a sense of enjoyment; you should develop it endowed with equanimity.

"When this concentration is thus developed, thus well-developed by you, you should train yourself: 'I will remain focused on feelings in & of themselves .... the mind in & of itself ... mental qualities in & of themselves—ardent, alert, & mindful—putting aside greed & distress with reference to the world.' That's how you should train yourself. When you have developed this concentration in this way, you should develop this concentration with directed thought & evaluation, you should develop it with no directed thought & a modicum of evaluation, you should develop it with no directed thought & no evaluation, you should develop it accompanied by rapture ... not accompanied by rapture ... endowed with a sense of enjoyment; you should develop it endowed with equanimity.

"When this concentration is thus developed, thus well-developed by you, then wherever you go, you will go in comfort. Wherever you stand, you will stand in comfort. Wherever you sit, you will sit in comfort. Wherever you lie down, you will lie down in comfort."

Then that monk, having been admonished by the admonishment from the Blessed One, got up from his seat and bowed down to the Blessed One, circled around him, keeping the Blessed One to his right side, and left. Then, dwelling alone, secluded, heedful, ardent, & resolute, he in no long time reached & remained in the supreme goal of the holy life for which clansmen rightly go forth from home into homelessness, knowing & realizing it for himself in the here & now. He knew: "Birth is ended, the holy life fulfilled, the task done. There is nothing further for the sake of this world." And thus he became another one of the Arahants.

—AN VIII.63

"Having abandoned the five hindrances—imperfections of awareness that weaken discernment—the monk remains focused on the body in & of itself—ardent, alert, & mindful—putting aside greed & distress with reference to the world. He remains focused on feelings...mind...mental qualities in & of themselves—ardent, alert, & mindful—

putting aside greed & distress with reference to the world. Just as if an elephant trainer were to plant a large post in the ground and were to bind a forest elephant to it by the neck in order to break it of its forest habits, its forest memories & resolves, its distraction, fatigue, & fever over leaving the forest, to make it delight in the town and to inculcate in it habits congenial to human beings; in the same way, these four frames of reference are bindings for the awareness of the disciple of the noble ones, to break him of his household habits, his household memories & resolves, his distraction, fatigue, & fever over leaving the household life, for the attainment of the right method and the realization of Unbinding.

"Then the Tathagata trains him further: 'Come, monk, remain focused on the body in & of itself, but do not think any thoughts connected with the body. Remain focused on feelings in & of themselves, but do not think any thoughts connected with feelings. Remain focused on the mind in & of itself, but do not think any thoughts connected with mind. Remain focused on mental qualities in & of themselves, but do not think any thoughts connected with mental qualities.' With the stilling of directed thought & evaluation, he enters the second jhana...."

—MN 125

"Monks, those who are new, not long gone-forth, only recently come to this doctrine & discipline, should be roused, encouraged, & exhorted by you to develop the four frames of reference [in this way]:

"'Come, friends, remain focused on the body in & of itself—being ardent, alert, with your minds unified, clear, concentrated, & single-minded for knowledge of the body as it actually is. Remain focused on feelings in & of themselves...focused on the mind in & of itself...focused on mental qualities in & of themselves—being ardent, alert, one-pointed, with your minds unified, clear, concentrated, & single-minded for knowledge of mental qualities as they actually are.'

"Monks, even those who are learners—who have yet to attain their hearts' desire, who stay resolved on the unsurpassed security from bondage—even they remain focused on the body in & of itself—being ardent, alert, one-pointed, with their minds unified, clear, concentrated, & single-minded for complete comprehension of the body. They remain focused on feelings in & of themselves...focused on the mind in & of itself...focused on mental qualities in & of themselves—being ardent, alert, one-pointed, with their minds unified, clear, concentrated, & single-minded for complete comprehension of mental qualities.

"Even those who are arahants—whose mental fermentations are ended, who have reached fulfillment, done the task, laid down the burden, attained the true goal, totally destroyed the fetter of becoming, and who are released through right gnosis—even they remain focused on the body in & of itself—being ardent, alert, one-pointed, with their minds unified, clear, concentrated, & single-minded, disjoined from the body. They remain focused on feelings in & of themselves...focused on the mind in & of itself...focused on mental qualities in & of themselves— being ardent, alert, one-pointed, with their minds unified, clear, concentrated, & single-minded, disjoined from mental qualities.

"So even those who are new, not long gone-forth, only recently come to this doctrine & discipline, should be roused, encouraged, & exhorted by you to develop the four frames of reference [in this way]."

—SN XLVII.4

"Suppose that there is a foolish, inexperienced, unskillful cook who has presented a king or a king's minister with various kinds of curry: mainly sour, mainly bitter, mainly peppery, mainly sweet, alkaline or non-alkaline, salty or non-salty. He does not take note of (lit: pick up on the theme of) his master, thinking, 'Today my master likes this curry, or he reaches out for that curry, or he takes a lot of this curry, or he praises that curry'....As a result, he is not rewarded with clothing or wages or gifts. Why is that? Because the foolish, inexperienced, unskillful cook does not pick up on the theme of his own master.

"In the same way, there are cases where a foolish, inexperienced, unskillful monk remains focused on the body in & of itself—ardent, alert, & mindful—putting aside greed & distress with reference to the world. As he remains thus focused on the body in & of itself, his mind does not become concentrated, his defilements [Comm: the five Hindrances] are not abandoned. He does not take note of that fact (does not pick up on that theme). He remains focused on feelings in & of themselves...the mind in & of itself...mental qualities in & of themselves—ardent, alert, & mindful—putting aside greed & distress with reference to the world. As he remains thus focused on mental qualities in & of themselves, his mind does not become concentrated, his defilements are not abandoned. He does not take note of that fact. As a result, he is not rewarded with a pleasant abiding here & now, nor with mindfulness & alertness. Why is that? Because the foolish, inexperienced, unskillful monk does not take note of his own mind (does not pick up on the theme of his own mind).

"Now suppose that there is a wise, experienced, skillful cook who has presented a king or a king's minister with various kinds of curry....He takes note of his master, thinking, 'Today my master likes this curry, or he reaches out for that curry, or he takes a lot of this curry or he praises that curry'....As a result, he is rewarded with clothing, wages, & gifts. Why is that? Because the wise, experienced, skillful cook picks up on the theme of his own master.

"In the same way, there are cases where a wise, experienced, skillful monk remains focused on the body in & of itself...feelings in & of themselves...the mind in & of itself...mental qualities in & of themselves—ardent, alert, & mindful—putting aside greed & distress with reference to the world. As he remains thus focused on mental qualities in & of themselves, his mind becomes concentrated, his defilements are abandoned. He takes note of that fact. As a result, he is rewarded with a pleasant abiding here & now, together with mindfulness & alertness. Why is that? Because the wise, experienced, skillful monk picks up on the theme of his own mind."

—SN XLVII.8

"Ananda, if a monk or nun remains with mind well established in the four frames of reference, he/she may be expected to realize greater-than-ever distinction.

"There is the case of a monk who remains focused on the body in & of itself—ardent, alert, & mindful—putting aside greed & distress with reference to the world. As he remains thus focused on the body in & of itself, a fever based on the body arises within his body, or there is sluggishness in his awareness, or his mind becomes scattered externally. He should then direct his mind to any inspiring theme [Comm: such as recollection of the Buddha]. As his mind is directed to any inspiring theme, delight arises within him. In one who feels delight, rapture arises. In one whose mind is enraptured, the body grows serene. His body serene, he feels pleasure. As he feels pleasure, his mind grows concentrated. He reflects, 'I have attained the aim to which my mind was directed. Let me withdraw [my mind from the inspiring theme].' He withdraws & engages neither in directed thought nor in evaluation. He discerns, 'I am not thinking or evaluating. I am inwardly mindful & at ease.'

"Furthermore, he remains focused on feelings...mind... mental qualities in & of themselves—ardent, alert, & mindful—putting aside greed & distress with reference to the world. As he remains thus focused on mental qualities in & of themselves, a fever based on mental qualities arises within his body, or there is sluggishness in his awareness, or his mind becomes scattered externally. He should then direct his mind to any inspiring theme. As his mind is directed to any inspiring theme, delight arises within him. In one who feels delight, rapture arises. In one whose mind is enraptured, the body grows serene. His body serene, he is sensitive to pleasure. As he feels pleasure, his mind grows concentrated. He reflects, 'I have attained the aim to which my mind was directed. Let me withdraw.' He withdraws & engages neither in directed thought nor in evaluation. He discerns, 'I am not thinking or evaluating. I am inwardly mindful & at ease.'

"This, Ananda, is development based on directing. And what is development based on not directing? A monk, when not directing his mind to external things, discerns, 'My mind is not directed to external things. It is not attentive to what is in front or behind. It is released & undirected. And furthermore I remain focused on the body in & of itself. I am ardent, alert, mindful, & at ease.'

"When not directing his mind to external things, he discerns, 'My mind is not directed to external things. It is not attentive to what is in front or behind. It is released & undirected. And furthermore I remain focused on feelings... mind...mental qualities in & of themselves. I am ardent, alert, mindful, & at ease.'

"This, Ananda, is development based on not directing.

"Now, Ananda, I have taught you development based on directing and development based on not directing. What a teacher should do out of compassion for his disciples, seeking their welfare, that I have done for you. Over there are [places to sit at] the foot of trees. Over there are empty dwellings. Practice jhana, Ananda. Do not be heedless. Do not be remorseful in the future. That is our instruction to you all."

—*SN XLVII.10*

VII. Jhana / Discernment

There is   no jhana
for one with   no discernment,
                 no discernment
for one with   no jhana.
But one with   both jhana
                 & discernment:
        he's on the verge
                 of Unbinding.

—*Dhp 372*

[Jhana as a prerequisite for liberating insight:] "If a monk would wish, 'May I—with the ending of mental fermentations—remain in the fermentation-free awareness-release & discernment-release, having directly known & realized them for myself right in the here-&-now,' then he should be one who brings the precepts to perfection, who is committed to mental calm, who does not neglect jhana, who is endowed with insight, and who frequents empty dwellings.

—*AN X.71*

"Monks, Sariputta is wise, of great discernment, deep discernment, wide ... joyous ... rapid ... quick ... penetrating discernment....There is the case where Sariputta...enters & remains in the first jhana. Whatever qualities there are in the first jhana—applied thought, evaluation, rapture, pleasure, singleness of mind, contact, feeling, perception, intention, consciousness (*vl.* intent), desire, decision, persistence, mindfulness, equanimity, & attention—he ferrets them out one by one. Known to him they arise, known to him they remain, known to him they subside. He discerns, 'So this is how these qualities, not having been, come into play. Having been, they vanish.' He remains unattracted & unrepelled with regard to those qualities, independent, detached, released, dissociated, with an awareness rid of barriers. He understands, 'There is a further escape,' and pursuing it, he confirms that 'There is.' (Similarly with the levels of jhana up through the sphere of nothingness.)

"Furthermore, completely transcending the sphere of nothingness, he enters & remains in the sphere of neither perception nor non-perception. He emerges mindful from that attainment. On emerging...he regards the past qualities that have ceased & changed: 'So this is how these qualities, not having been, come into play. Having been, they vanish.' He remains unattracted & unrepelled with regard to those qualities, independent, detached, released, dissociated, with an awareness rid of barriers. He understands, 'There is a further escape,' and pursuing it, he confirms that 'There is.'

"Furthermore, completely transcending the sphere of neither perception nor non-perception, he enters & remains in the cessation of feeling & perception. When he sees with discernment, his fermentations are totally ended. He emerges mindful from that attainment. On emerging...he regards the past qualities that have ceased & changed: 'So this is how these qualities, not having been, come into play. Having been, they vanish.' He remains unattracted & unrepelled with regard to those qualities, independent, detached, released, dissociated, with an awareness rid of barriers. He understands, 'There is no further escape,' and pursuing it, he confirms that 'There isn't.'

"If someone, rightly describing a person, were to say, 'He has attained mastery & perfection in noble virtue... noble concentration...noble discernment...noble release,' he would be rightly describing Sariputta.... Sariputta takes the unexcelled wheel of Dhamma set rolling by the Tathagata, and keeps it rolling rightly."

—MN 111

"I tell you, the ending of the fermentations depends on the first jhana...the second jhana...the third...the fourth...the sphere of the infinitude of space...the sphere of the infinitude of consciousness...the sphere of nothingness...the sphere of neither perception nor non-perception.

"'I tell you, the ending of the fermentations depends on the first jhana.' Thus it has been said. In reference to what was it said?... Suppose that an archer or archer's apprentice were to practice on a straw man or mound of clay, so that after a while he would become able to shoot long distances, to fire accurate shots in rapid succession, and to pierce great masses. In the same way, there is the case where a monk...enters & remains in the first jhana: rapture & pleasure born of withdrawal, accompanied by directed thought & evaluation. He regards whatever phenomena there that are connected with form, feeling, perceptions, fabrications, & consciousness, as inconstant, stressful, a disease, a cancer, an arrow, painful, an affliction, alien, a disintegration, a void, not-self. He turns his mind away from those phenomena, and having done so, inclines his mind to the property of deathlessness: 'This is peace, this is exquisite—the resolution of all fabrications; the relinquishment of all acquisitions; the ending of craving; dispassion; cessation; Unbinding.'

"Staying right there, he reaches the ending of the mental fermentations. Or, if not, then through this very Dhamma-passion, this Dhamma-delight, and through the total wasting away of the five lower fetters [self-identity views, grasping at precepts & practices, uncertainty, sensual passion, and irritation]—he is due to be reborn [in the Pure Abodes], there to be totally unbound, never again to return from that world.

"'I tell you, the ending of the fermentations depends on the first jhana.' Thus it was said, and in reference to this was it said."

[Similarly with the other levels of jhana up through the sphere of nothingness.]

"Thus, as far as the perception-attainments go, that is as far as gnosis-penetration goes. As for these two spheres—the attainment of the sphere of neither perception nor non-perception & the attainment of the cessation of feeling & perception—I tell you that they are to be rightly explained by those monks who are meditators, skilled in attaining, skilled in attaining & emerging, who have attained & emerged in dependence on them."

—AN IX.36

Then Dasama the householder from the city of Atthaka went to where Ven. Ananda was staying and on arrival, having bowed down, sat to one side. As he was sitting there, he said to Ven. Ananda, "Is there, venerable sir, any one condition explained by the Blessed One...whereby a monk—dwelling heedful, ardent, & resolute—releases his mind that is as yet unreleased, or whereby the fermentations not yet brought to an end come to an end, or whereby he attains the unsurpassed security from bondage that he has not yet attained?"

Ananda: "Yes, householder, there is....There is the case where a monk...enters & remains in the first jhana....He notices that 'This first jhana is fabricated & willed.' He discerns, 'Whatever is fabricated & willed is inconstant & subject to cessation.' Staying right there, he reaches the ending of the fermentations. Or, if not, then through this very Dhamma-passion, this Dhamma-delight, and through the total wasting away of the five lower fetters, he is due to be reborn [in the Pure Abodes], there to be totally unbound, never again to return from that world."

[Similarly with the other levels of jhana up through the sphere of nothingness and the four awareness-releases based on good will, compassion, appreciation, & equanimity.]

—AN XI.17

Sariputta: "This Unbinding is pleasant, friends. This Unbinding is pleasant."

Udayin: "But what is the pleasure here, my friend, where there is nothing felt?"

Sariputta: "Just that is the pleasure here, my friend: where there is nothing felt. There are these five strands of sensuality. Which five? Forms cognizable via the eye—agreeable, pleasing, charming, endearing, fostering desire, enticing; sounds ... smells ... tastes ... tactile sensations cognizable via the body—agreeable, pleasing, charming, endearing, fostering desire, enticing. Whatever pleasure or joy arises in dependence on these five strands of sensuality, that is sensual pleasure.

"Now there is the case where a monk—quite withdrawn from sensuality, withdrawn from unskillful qualities—enters & remains in the first jhana....If, as he remains there, he is beset with attention to perceptions dealing with *sensuality*, that is an affliction for him. Just as pain arises as an affliction for a healthy person, even so the attention to perceptions dealing with sensuality that beset the monk is an affliction for him. Now the Blessed One has said that whatever is an affliction is stress. So by this line of reasoning it may be known how Unbinding is pleasant.

"Furthermore, there is the case where a monk...enters & remains in the second jhana....If, as he remains there, he is beset with attention to perceptions dealing with *directed thought*, that is an affliction for him....

"Furthermore, there is the case where a monk...enters & remains in the third jhana....If, as he remains there, he is beset with attention to perceptions dealing with *rapture,* that is an affliction for him....

"Furthermore, there is the case where a monk...enters & remains in the fourth jhana....If, as he remains there, he is beset with attention to perceptions dealing with *equanimity,* that is an affliction for him....

"Furthermore, there is the case where a monk...enters & remains in the sphere of the infinitude of space. If, as he remains there, he is beset with attention to perceptions dealing with *form,* that is an affliction for him....

"Furthermore, there is the case where a monk...enters & remains in the sphere of the infinitude of consciousness. If, as he remains there, he is beset with attention to perceptions dealing with *the sphere of the infinitude of space,* that is an affliction for him....

"Furthermore, there is the case where a monk...enters & remains in the sphere of nothingness. If, as he remains there, he is beset with attention to perceptions dealing with *the sphere of the infinitude of consciousness,* that is an affliction for him....

"Furthermore, there is the case where a monk...enters & remains in the sphere of neither perception nor non-perception. If, as he remains there, he is beset with attention to perceptions dealing with *the sphere of the infinitude of consciousness,* that is an affliction for him...whatever is an affliction is stress. So by this line of reasoning it may be known how Unbinding is pleasant.

"Furthermore, there is the case where a monk...enters & remains in the cessation of perception & feeling. And, having seen [that] with discernment, his fermentations are completely ended. So by this line of reasoning it may be known how Unbinding is pleasant."

—*AN IX.34*

"[On attaining the fourth level of jhana] there remains only equanimity: pure & bright, pliant, malleable & luminous. Just as if a skilled goldsmith or goldsmith's apprentice were to prepare a furnace, heat up a crucible, and, taking gold with a pair of tongs, place it in the crucible. He would blow on it periodically, sprinkle water on it periodically, examine it periodically, so that the gold would become refined, well-refined, thoroughly refined, flawless, free from dross, pliant, malleable & luminous. Then whatever sort of ornament he had in mind—whether a belt, an earring, a necklace, or a gold chain—it would serve his purpose. In the same way, there remains only equanimity: pure & bright, pliant, malleable, & luminous. He [the meditator] discerns that 'If I were to direct equanimity as pure & bright as this toward the dimension of the infinitude of space, I would develop the mind along those lines, and thus this equanimity of mine—thus supported, thus sustained—would last for a long time. (Similarly with the dimensions of the infinitude of consciousness, nothingness, & neither perception nor non-perception.)'

"He discerns that 'If I were to direct equanimity as pure & bright as this toward the dimension of the infinitude of space and to develop the mind along those lines, that would be fabricated. (Similarly with the dimensions of the infinitude of consciousness, nothingness, & neither perception nor non-perception.)' He neither fabricates nor wills for the sake of becoming or un-becoming. This being the case, he is not sustained by anything in the world (does not cling to anything in the world). Unsustained, he is not agitated. Unagitated, he is totally unbound right within. He discerns that 'Birth is ended, the holy life fulfilled, the task done. There is nothing further for this world.'"

—MN 140

"Further, Ananda, the monk—not attending to the perception of wilderness, not attending to the perception of earth—attends to the singleness based on the perception of the dimension of the infinitude of space. His mind takes pleasure, finds satisfaction, settles, & indulges in its perception of the dimension of the infinitude of space.

"He discerns that 'Whatever disturbances that would exist based on the perception of wilderness are not present. Whatever disturbances that would exist based on the perception of earth are not present. There is only this modicum of disturbance: the singleness based on the perception of the dimension of the infinitude of space.' He discerns that 'This mode of perception is empty of the perception of wilderness. This mode of perception is empty of the perception of earth. There is only this non-emptiness: the singleness based on the perception of the dimension of the infinitude of space.' Thus he regards it as empty of whatever is not there. Whatever remains, he discerns as present: 'There is this.' And so this, his entry into emptiness, accords with actuality, is undistorted in meaning, & pure.

"Further, Ananda, the monk—not attending to the perception of earth, not attending to the perception of the dimension of the infinitude of space—attends to the singleness based on the perception of the dimension of the infinitude of consciousness. His mind takes pleasure, finds satisfaction, settles, & indulges in its perception of the dimension of the infinitude of consciousness.

"He discerns that 'Whatever disturbances that would exist based on the perception of earth are not present. Whatever disturbances that would exist based on the perception of the dimension of the infinitude of space are not present. There is only this modicum of disturbance: the singleness based on the perception of the dimension of the infinitude of consciousness.' He discerns that 'This mode of perception is empty of the perception of earth. This mode of perception is empty of the perception of the dimension of the infinitude of space. There is only this non-emptiness: the singleness based on the perception of the dimension of the infinitude of consciousness.' Thus he regards it as empty of whatever is not there. Whatever remains, he discerns as present: 'There is this.' And so this, his entry into emptiness, accords with actuality, is undistorted in meaning, & pure.

[Similarly with the dimension of nothingness and the dimension of neither perception nor non-perception.]

"Further, Ananda, the monk—not attending to the perception of the dimension of nothingness, not attending to the perception of the dimension of neither perception nor non-perception—attends to the singleness based on the theme-less concentration of awareness. His mind takes pleasure, finds satisfaction, settles, & indulges in its theme-less concentration of awareness.

"He discerns that 'Whatever disturbances would exist based on the perception of the dimension of nothingness are not present. Whatever disturbances would exist based on the perception of the dimension of neither perception nor non-perception, are not present. And there is only this modicum of disturbance: that connected with the six sensory spheres, dependent on this very body with life as its condition.' He discerns that 'This mode of perception is empty of the perception of the dimension of nothingness. This mode of perception is empty of the perception of the dimension of neither perception nor non-perception. There is only this non-emptiness: that connected with the six sensory spheres, dependent on this very body with life as its condition.' Thus he regards it as empty of whatever is not there. Whatever remains, he discerns as present: 'There is this.' And so this, his entry into emptiness, accords with actuality, is undistorted in meaning, & pure.

"Further, Ananda, the monk—not attending to the perception of the dimension of nothingness, not attending to the perception of the dimension of neither perception nor non-perception—attends to the singleness based on the theme-less concentration of awareness. His mind takes pleasure, finds satisfaction, settles, & indulges in its theme-less concentration of awareness.

"He discerns that 'This theme-less concentration of awareness is fabricated & mentally fashioned.' And he discerns that 'Whatever is fabricated & mentally fashioned is inconstant & subject to cessation.' For him—thus knowing, thus seeing—the mind is released from the fermentation of sensuality, the fermentation of becoming, the fermentation of ignorance. With release, there is the knowledge, 'Released.' He discerns that 'Birth is ended, the holy life fulfilled, the task done. There is nothing further for this world.'

"He discerns that 'Whatever disturbances would exist based on the fermentation of sensuality...the fermentation of becoming...the fermentation of ignorance, are not present. And there is only this modicum of disturbance: that connected with the six sensory spheres, dependent on this very body with life as its condition.' He discerns that 'This mode of perception is empty of the fermentation of sensuality ... becoming ... ignorance. And there is just this non-emptiness: that connected with the six sensory spheres, dependent on this very body with life as its condition.' Thus he regards it as empty of whatever is not there. Whatever remains, he discerns as present: 'There is this.' And so this, his entry into emptiness, accords with actuality, is undistorted in meaning, pure—superior & unsurpassed."

—MN 121

Glossary

Abhidhamma: The third of the three "baskets" or collections that comprise the Pali Canon, devoted to establishing the precise taxonomy of the terms found in the other two collections. Generally believed to be a later addition to the Canon.

Āsava: Fermentation; effluent. The mind has four types of fermentation: sensual passion, views, becoming, and ignorance.

Arahant: "Worthy one; pure one." A person who has mastered the kamma that puts an end to kamma, and thus is not destined for future rebirth.

Bodhisatta: A being destined for Awakening. After his Awakening, the Buddha used this term to refer to himself prior to his Awakening.

Dhamma: (1) Event; action; (2) a phenomenon in and of itself; (3) mental quality; (4) doctrine, teaching; (5) *nibbāna* (although there are passages describing nibbāna as the abandoning of all dhammas). Sanskrit form: Dharma.

Jhāna: Mental absorption. A state of strong concentration focused on a single sensation or mental notion. This term is related to the verb *jhāyati,* which means to burn with a still, steady flame.

Kamma: Intentional act. Sanskrit form: Karma.

Nibbāna: Literally, the "unbinding" of the mind from passion, aversion, and delusion, and from the entire round of death and rebirth. As this term also denotes the extinguishing of a fire, it carries connotations of stilling, cooling, and peace. "Total nibbāna" in some contexts denotes the experience of Awakening; in others, the final passing away of an arahant. Sanskrit form: Nirvāṇa.

Sangha: The Community of the Buddha's followers. This term has two levels of meaning. On the conventional level it refers to ordained monks and nuns. On the ideal level, it refers to all those—lay or ordained—who have reached at least the first of the four levels of Awakening.

Sutta: Discourse.

Tathāgata: Literally, "one who has become authentic (*tatha-āgata*)," an epithet used in ancient India for a person who has attained the highest religious goal. In Buddhism, it usually denotes the Buddha, although occasionally it also denotes any of his arahant disciples.

Further Reading

For further reading on contemplation of the body, see the following books and dhamma talks available on Access to Insight (www.accesstoinsight.org):

Ajaan Mun Bhuridatto: *A Heart Released*

Ajaan Mun Bhuridatto: *The Ever-present Truth*

Ajaan Lee Dhammadharo: *The Craft of the Heart*

Ajaan Lee Dhammadharo: *Frames of Reference*

Ajaan Maha Boowa Ñanasampanno: "The Work of a Contemplative"

Ajaan Maha Boowa Ñanasampanno: "An Heir to the Dhamma"

Ajaan Suwat Suvaco: "This Body of Mine"

Ajaan Suwat Suvaco: "Disenchantment"

For supplemental reading on the issues of jhana, mindfulness, and insight, see the articles, "The Path of Mindfulness and Concentration" and "One Tool Among Many," also available on Access to Insight.